Economic Transition Indian Industrial Performance

Economic Transition Indian Industrial Performance

Dr Rajendra Prathipati

KALPAZ

First Published, 2018

Published by

Kalpaz Publications
C-30, Satyawati Nagar,
Delhi – 110052
E-mail: kalpaz@hotmail.com
Ph.: 9212142040

Printed at: G. Print Process, Delhi

Cataloging in Publication Data—DK
Courtesy: D.K. Agencies (P) Ltd. <docinfo@dkagencies.com>

Prathpati, Rajendra, author.
Economic transition Indian industrial performance / Dr Rajendra Prathipati.
pages cm
Includes bibliographical references.
ISBN 9789386397249 (HB)

1. Manufacturing industries—India. 2. Manufacturing industries—Government policy—India. I. Title.

LCC HD9736.I52P73 2018 | DDC 338.47670954 23

Contents

Foreword 9

Preface 11

Acknowledgements 15

1. Industrial Scenario in Transition - An Overview 17

• Introduction • External and internal Pressures • Economic Openness and Economic Prosperity • Structural Changes in the Industrial Sector • The Total Factor Productivity [TFP] factor • Empirical Studies Related to the Inter-Relationship [Economic Openness and (Technical Efficiency) Industrial Performance] • Analytical Framework • Objectives of the Study • Hypothesis • Methodology • Organization of the Study • References.

2. Evaluation of Industrial Policies 57

• Introduction • Circumstances during NIP • Industrial Policy Regime • Industrial Licensing • Foreign Investment • Foreign Technology • Public Sector Role • Monopolies and Restrictive Trade Practices Act (MRTP) • Industrial location policy liberalized • Abolition of Phased-Manufacturing Programmes [new projects] • Removal of mandatory convertibility clause • Appraisal of New Industrial Policy • Boosting Manufacturing Sector [Other major policies] • References.

3. Growth Performance Analysis [Domestic Industries under Technological Classification] 73

• IntroductionGrowth Performance Analysis • GPA at Macro-level • International level comparison [GDP and Employment]; • Trends in Export of Indian Manufacturing Sector • Growth Performance Analysis of Technology Based Classification • Growth Rates of Gross Value Added, Capital and Labour in High Technology Manufacturing Sector • Growth Rates of Gross Value Added, Capital and Labour in Medium High Technology Manufacturing Sector • Growth Performance Analysis of Technology Based Classification • Growth Rates of Gross Value Added, Capital and Labour in Low Technology Manufacturing Sector • Growth Rates of Gross Value Added, Capital and Labour in Medium Low Technology Manufacturing Sector.

4. Economic Openness Impact [Pre and Post-Transition] 91

• Methodology Framework • Malmquist Total Factor Productivity (TFP) Index • Empirical Findings • TFP Trends - High-technology Manufacturing Sector • TFP Trends - Medium High-technology Manufacturing Sector • TFP Trends - Low-Technology Manufacturing Sector • TFP Trends - Medium Low Technology Manufacturing Sector • References.

5. Conclusion and Recommendations 125

• Findings of the Study • Growth Performance Analysis • Industry-wise findings - TFPG and Sources • Recommendations and Policy implications.

Bibilography 133

Appendices 143

Index 169

Dedicated To
my God
Prince of Peace
and
My beloved Parents
Prathipati Ramesh, Veeramma

Foreword

The study conducted by **Dr. Rajendra Prathipati** is of great contemporary relevance in the context of every country being seized of liberalization. Economic openness is considered ***"sine qua non"*** for industrial growth. In the situation of economic progress slowing down, even in countries like USA and RUSSIA at just 1.9 percent during 2017-18, there is a greater concern expressed on the strategies to promote growth. Imminently, it is the industrial sector that is thought of as the saviour. For the past few years, newly industrialized nations (So called developing economies) are excelling in their performance over the developed nations. While the developed countries, since the turn of the present country, registering a growth rate of just 2-3 percent on average, developing countries are able to progress by about 4-5 percent. Countries like China, South Korea, Singapore and India proved to be an exception with their scintilling growth record.

In respect of India, the growth story is quite impressive since the beginning of the nineties of the 20th country. India has just celebrated its 70th Independence (having secured freedom on August 15, 1947) with astounding confidence and resounding success. After the period of seventy years, Indian economy could register a growth rate of about 3.5 percent on an average. It is by no means a mean achievement. Its growth has gallopped since the launching of the first phase of economic reforms since 1991-92. The country could register a consistent progress with about 6.0percent during nineties, 7.0 percent during the turn of the 21st country and beyond this threshold limit now. It is a matter of gratification to cite the observation of the international monotony fund (IMF) that India has been in a strong hold of recording 7.2 percent growth rate in 2017-18 and 7.7 percent in 2018-19, overtaking the neighboring china, which is expected to record only 6.7 percent and 6.4 percent in the two reference years.

It is in this context, the study conducted by **Dr.Rajendra. P.** assumes further significance. What all, India could achieve, need to be ascribed to the openness of the economy. It is implicit in saying that economic openness makes the industry more efficient, productive and vibrant. The 'make in India' agenda of the present government in power is aimed at strengthring the Indian manufacturing sector, by inviting companies across the world. It is also implicit in the process to utilize the highly talented and skilled human resources available in India to produce goods and services of the international standand. The coverage of the scheme is extended to include twenty five sectors of the Indian industry. In order to be also to realize the goal, the government of India has also formulated a new foreign direct investment policy (FDI), opening up a wide verity of sectors, including defence and retailing. And most of the permissions are processed through **"Automatic route".**

Dr. Rajendra has employed the time tested methodology, by using total factor productivity (TFP) to highlight the impact of openness prevailing in the country. His classification of industries into four categories, high, medium high, medium low and low technology is highly appropriate. Considering gross value added (GVA) in place of GDP is also in the fitness of contemporary thinking. Nonetheless to state that the findings of the study deserve attention of the economists and policy makers an equal footing. That openness contributes significantly to the growth of all kinds of industries, irrespective of the intensity of the technology employed and dynamism, is amply proved.

I congratulate **Dr.Rajendra Prathipati** for having conducted a painstaking, incisive and Indepth analysis of the factors contributing to the growth and performance of Indian industry. I wish him good luck.

Professor K. Viyyanna Rao
Former vice –Chancellor
Acharya Nagarjuna
University
Andhra Pradesh

Date:- 18.08.2017

Preface

The manufacturing Industrial sector is the fulcrum that determines the path's of economy's progress. It reflects the progress of knowledge economy and the economic discipline among its economic agents that a developing economy passes through. Raj Krishna's 3.5% Hindu rate of growth raised more questions about the viability and sustainability of the Indian economy's growth and the sectoral growth rate contributions. Srimati Indira Gandhi's subsequent focus on productivity and the Seventh Plan objectives on 'Food, Work and Productivity' during Shri Rajiv Gandhi's time were the building blocks of productivity thinking in India. The subsequent failures of the Indian economy resulting in twin deficits i.e. Balance of Payment Deficit and the Fiscal deficit along with other structural features brought in the LPG (Liberalization, Privatization and Globalization) reforms of 1991-92.

Professor Deepak Nayyar of the Jawaharlal Nehru University in a crucial paper on 'India's Unfinished Journey: From Growth to Development' was unequivocal in pointing out the turning points of Indian economy and put 1980-81 and not 1991-92. Mr Rajendra Prathipati's work on 'Impact of Economic Openness on Industrial Efficiency: A Study on transition in Indian Manufacturing Sector' has taken one of the breakpoints as 1980-81. While his focus on structural thinking in manufacturing sector reveals a conviction that 1991-92 can be cited as the time point where Indian economy opened up. So he wanted to study what he considers pre openness and post openness time frames; openness being defined in terms of liberalization process initiated in that year.

Dr Pratipathi's key focus was to assess possible links in Liberalization and Productivity, since the latter is taken as a driving force for growth and technological progress. Liberalization, he believed, would open up the forces of competition and would force firms to be more technically efficient by increasing organizational competence, L skills, capacity utilization and enhance innovation. Liberalization is also a precursor to globalization as without the former, foreign players would suffer from trust deficit in the trajectories of the Indian economy.

The author has taken a technological classification approach of the OECD:2003 as the Indian science and technology Policy (ISTP)-2001 recognized the role of technology to encourage R&D Innovation in the economy. He divided the industrial manufacturing sector into four categories: i-High Technology Industries ii-Medium High Technology Industries iii- Medium Low Technology Industries and iv-low Technology Industries. The period with 1991 as break point provided him with a handle to divide his study into two time periods: pre 1991 (1980-91) and post 1991 (1991-2012). Author cites Bai and Perror Methodology-2003 for simultaneous estimation of multiple breakpoints. He conducted the study after doing due concordance analysis. Then a Malmquist Productivity Index method were used to calculate Total Factor Productivity (TFP) of the Indian manufacturing sector.

The study is divided into six chapters. While the third Chapter on Policy could have been further refined, Chapter Four is spot on in analyzing the growth performance of Indian Manufacturing Sector in pre and post transition periods for different industries group wise and individually. Chapter Five looked into the efficiency (defined in terms of productivity here) using Malmquist Data envelopment Analysis for selected Industry Groups for different periods. Chapter Six moved into a summary and findings to generate policy suggestions for Manufacturing as a whole and selected Industries in particular.

A quick look at the results is outlined here.

Growth performance of High Technology Sector showed that trend in Gross Value Added has been positive along with growth rate of Capital. But growth rate of Labor shows negative visa vis pre transition period. The highest growth rate of Radio, TV and Communication industry showed how ICT has been a driver of growth in Indian economy. But drugs and Medicines was not doing well along with the lowest Labor growth rate.

In Medium High Technology Manufacturing Sector, almost all industries recorded downturn in Capital and Labor. However, Chemicals and Drugs had shown an interesting statistics that Labor gr rate has shown an upturn. This was crucial for later growth of pharma sector as knowledge instincts has begun to capture the labor force and this would show results later. [The author does not discuss this as this is beyond the scope of the current work.]

In the Low technology Manufacturing Sector, it was heartening that Food Beverages and Tobacco showed high growth of capital in the post transition period. This was despite the 2008 Global Depression and when both Manufacturing and Aggregative Growth was dipping. But other Labor Intensive Industries did not show increase in growth rates, a sign of immaturity and where government needs to work. This has subsequently given rise to Prime Minister Modi's Make in India programmes, etc.

Trends in TFP showed positive growth in post transition period and more so in Communication sector. Medium and High technology Manufacturing showed both technological change and technical Change contributed to TFP. In low Technology Manufacturing Sector showed positive contribution from technical change but not so from technological change. But in Medium Low Technology Manufacturing Sector showed main source of TFPG is due to technological change. On an aggregate, technological change is greater than technical efficiency that showed that TFP increase was due to frontier shifts which can be attributed to Openness in the Indian Economy.

This work is an useful contribution to TFPG and shows positive links between Openness (Liberalization) but sectoral shortfalls can be attributed to implementation issues that has largely been the bane of Independent India and that the Current regime is trying to redeem.

Debasis Patnaik, Ph.D.

Faculty, BITS Pilani, K K Birla Goa Campus

Goa-403726

Acknowledgements

"I will give thanks to the LORD with my whole heart; I will tell of all thy wonderful deeds" (Psalm 9:1)

I express my heartfelt thanks and a deep sense of gratitude to my supervisor - Prof. Boppana Nagarjuna, School of Economics, University of Hyderabad for his constant help and guidance at every stage of my doctoral research.

I extend my gratitude to Prof. G. Nancharaiah (Former Vice-Chancellor, Babasaheb Bhimrao Ambedkar University, Lucknow) School of Economics, University of Hyderabad and all the faculty members of the department, School of Economics especially Prof. Somayajulu, Prof. B. Kamaiah, Prof. Vijay for their constant support and encouragement during my studies at University of Hyderabad.

I am deeply indebted to Prof. Tim Coelli, Centre for Efficiency and Productivity Analysis, University of New England, Australia, who provided a computer software "Data Envelopment Analysis Program Version 2.1" online services for analyzing my research data.

My heart felt gratitude to Prof. Debasis Patnaik (Head of the Department of Economics, BITS-Pilani, K. K. Birla Goa Campus) in spite of his busy schedule, for readily accepting my requisition and read the formal thesis thoroughly and gave his comments. As an eminent scholar of this field and on the productivity and its application, analysis of the Industrial Sector in India and the west, I am greatly delighted for his gift of preface ornament to this book.

And, My sincere thanks to My friends who is a great source of inspiration, Dr. Francis Rathinam, Senior Evaluation Specialist at 3ie (International Initiative for Impact Evaluation) org, Prince Matthew

Thomas (Sr Deputy Editor at Business Line), Roop Kumar and Dr. Ravi Prakash.

My sincere thanks to the Acharya Nagarjuna University authorities (then and now) and the Staff, especially Sarath Chandra and Krishnaiah (Library Assistants) Lakshman (Asst. Registrar), Kanaka Sundaram (Addl. Controller of Examinations), Narasa Reddy (Asst. Registrar), Pulla Rao, Prakash, Bahnu, Appi Reddy, Yobu,Yesu, Mohan Rao, Rajashekar, Ravi Chandra and Lakshman CDE, Ch. Sambaiah, Sr. Asst, Acharya Nagarjuna University.

My special thanks to my friends whose ideas and knowledge shaped my preliminary thoughts into a solid state on the work – Dr.Vijay Kumar, Ch. Raju, Ganga Raju, Dr.Madukar, who helped in my research work and also my Postgraduate classmates Dr.Chandiah, Dr.Jagadeesh, Shyam, Dr.Sowmya, Dr.Itisree, Ancy, Sruthi. And, my seniors- Dr.Muni Swamy, Dr.Steeven Raj, Dr.Gurajala Ravi, Dr.Venugopal and Ajay.

My heartfelt thanks to my family members. It is my pleasure to remember my grandparents Prattipati Paul and Tulasamma for their thirst for education and encouraging me to achieve this goal. I am very much indebted to my beloved parents – Ramesh (father) and Veeramma (mother) whose sacrificial life made me to be the part of this academic world to reach this stage with successful life. I thank to God for them. My deepest thanks to my loving sisters, Suneetha, Prasanna Leela, Mercy Swarna Lata and and thier kids Princy, Praisy and Lincy. I also express my gratitude to Dr. Matthew Prattipati, Chief Resource Person (Academic), at National Translation Mission, Central Institute of Indian Languages, Manasagangotri, Mysuru,Karnataka State and my aunt C Devi Janett always encouraging me in my studies and praying for my family.

Above all, my heart full thanks to my wife Rajakumari for her continuous support, love and affection and also my blessed sons- Prince Rozen and Vincen Roger.

Rajendra Prathipati

Acharya Nagarjuna University
GUNTUR-Andhra Pradesh

Chapter - I

Industrial Scenario in Transition - An Overview

Introduction

Over the past three decades, *Economic Openness* has become an important part of many countries. It has witnessed revolutionary changes in the manufacturing sector at home and abroad. Most of the economists believed the economy to be in abyss, since independence. This problem trails over to the uncertainty over the past several years. The decade 1980's owes to large and persistent macro economic imbalances. The Balance of payments [BOP] situation was highly precarious, with appreciable inflationary pressures and inherent fiscal imbalances. The government at the Centre often decided to introduce Economic Openness[1].

The liberalized economic policies were initiated with the prevalent fiscal and balance of payment crisis. The gross fiscal deficit of the government at the Centre was up from 6.1 per cent to 8.4 per cent of the gross domestic product (GDP) ['80-'81 and '90-'91]. The fiscal deficit ought to be met by borrowing from the central bank and the public at large. Consequently, the internal debts [as a proportion of GDP] increased from 35.6 per cent to 53.5 per cent in the same period, whereas the interest payments doubled from two per cent to four per cent [of the GDP]. The balance of payment crisis was evident from the past that the current account deficit [as a proportion of GDP] almost doubled from 1.3 per cent to 2.2 per cent [of GDP] between early and the latter half of '80s, crossing over to three per cent in 1991. The piquant situation was noted by the then Finance Minister, "foreign reserves had dwindled to Rs.2, 600 core, barely sufficient for two weeks of import. International commercial banks refused to extend new credits. Large outflows followed from NRI deposits. Industrial growth receded on severe import squeeze with accelerated inflation. It looked as if the country's economic and financial system was jeopardized, leading to widespread unemployment, loss of output and the emergence of a higher inflationary spiral."[2] We have discussed the problems at home, ignoring some external pressures for Economic Openness.

External and internal Pressures

The government at the Centre was perforce to approach the international financial bodies such as the International Monetary Fund (IMF) and the World Bank (WB). However, the internal austerity measures were insufficient to bail the economic abyss out, wherein the country hung over. The institutions have agreed to extend standby credit and long-term support subject to the conditionality of India accepting the Structural Adjustment Program (SAP), under which it was obliged to commit for change in economic policies. The institutions have recommended a program package similar to that developed earlier for the Latin American and African countries. The institutional duo has worked out upon the diagnosis and the remedies, for sustained economic growth could help in productive employment and reduce poverty.

India moves towards more Economic Openness [LPG] on par with the reforms worldwide. A number of developing countries have turned to the market economy [appreciable rational allocation of resources for accelerated pace of economic development], on the balkanization of the erstwhile USSR. The end of the decade has found hastening of the trend. The developments at the international arena have also influenced our economy, calling for economic reforms [1991]. The gulf war owed to mid-1991s B.O.P besides the perpetual US fiscal deficits to have virtually influenced the country's economic policy.

The inevitable situation has alarmed the authorities introduce a two-pronged economic policy.

[1] Macro Economic Stabilization and [2] Structural Adjustment Policies

The stabilization usually refers to the IMF policies. It could be defined as the correction of unsustainable fiscal imbalances, whereas the policies of structural adjustment, on the other refer to the WB, leading for the medium-term assistance, reorienting the economy for greater efficiency. The World Bank defined the process as 'reforms of policies and institutions-micro economic (such as taxes), macroeconomic such as fixed imbalance and institutional public inefficiency.' In practice, the term has been defined variously. Analysts Corbo and Fischer have defined 'It as a process of market-oriented reforms in policies and institutions, with the goal of restoring a sustainable balance of payments, for sustainable growth in per capita income' (1995, p.2847)[3]. Other definitions carry the narrow structural adjustment to denote policies aimed at improving an economic efficiency and long-term growth.

The structural reforms broadly covered the areas of industrial licensing, foreign trade, foreign investment, exchange rate management and the financial sector. For the present study would like to focus particularly on "Impact of Economic Openness on Industrial Efficiency (productivity growth)". Below were being discussed the Economic Openness and Economic prosperity besides the existing industrial structure changes.

Economic Openness and Economic Prosperity

While theory and cross-country studies consensually suggest that economic openness increases overall welfare (details given in figure 1.1). The points below projects benefits accruing from Economic Openness.

Dissemination of knowledge and innovation embodied in goods, services and investments - Using a panel of over 23,000 European establishments 2007, Bloom et al. (2009) found, 'Chinese import competition led to both within firm technology upgrading, and between firm reallocation of employment towards more technologically intensive plants. These effects are growing over time as Chinese trade volumes raise, accounting for up to 38 per cent of technology upgrading in the

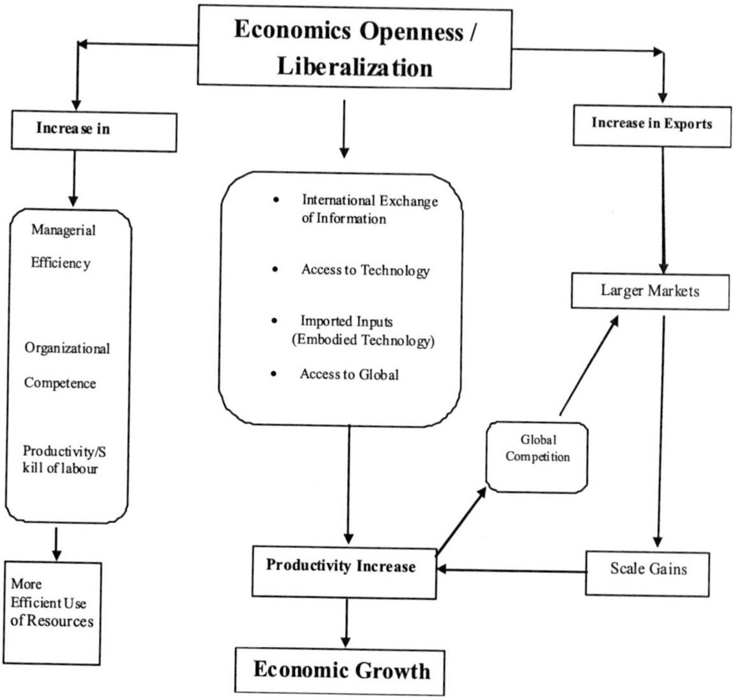

Sources: Srivastava, V (1996), Liberalisation, *Productivity and Competition: A Panel Study of Indian Manufacturing,* Oxford University Press, New Delhi.

Figure 1.1: Economic Openness (Liberalization) and Productivity-Possible Links*

---

* Note: Different researchers have tried to establish a possible link between Economic Openness (liberalization) and productivity .the process of liberalization would lead to more competition in an economy. This increase in competition would pressurize the firms to be technically efficient by increasing organizational competence, skills of the labour, capacity utilization and making the firms more innovative. This would probably result into more efficient use of resources. On the other hand, due to liberalization process i.e. second link establishes that would allow the firms to have international exchange of information, easy access to technology, imported inputs and access to global capital thereby, resulting into higher productivity gains and higher economic growth.

most recent years. These results suggest that imports from low wage countries appear to have potentially large beneficial impacts on technical change'.

Foreign investments contribute to economic prosperity - *Inward investments* may crowd out a small element of domestic investment, but the net result is to increase the capital stock of an economy, beneficial to growth and employment. The flows of investment enable the reallocation of resources to more efficient and productive activities. Inward FDI can be a useful vehicle for the transfer of innovative technologies and processes. It can have spill-over effects that work to boost the productivity of industry and wider economy linking with domestic firms. The conventional wisdom left for developing countries is that their benefits of inward investment depend on their reaching a threshold capacity in human capital and financial development. New evidence suggests the FDI impact on growth at the level of the firm remain systematically larger in low income countries than elsewhere[4]. *Investments abroad* can also bring important benefits to the home economy. If activities, where the comparative advantage lies elsewhere, are outsourced to more efficient locations, this can free up resources at home to undertake more productive activities. However that at the level of the firm, Oversea investment may generate export, for the foreign investor, who uses parts of established supplier chains in providing goods/services in the country, where they have invested. Investment in fast-growing economies and industries abroad often bring high returns, improving the balance of payments. The returns can be reinvested in higher-skilled activities in the domestic front, as firms often maintain their head office and research and development activities, while export in lower-skilled activities. Outward investment also provides a good route for technology transfer towards the home economy.

Enhanced competition for improved productivity - These dynamic effects will occur through allocative efficiency (reallocation of resources across firms and most importantly inside firms), productive efficiency (reduction of managerial slack and increases in workers' efforts), and dynamic efficiency (increase in innovation)[5]

Structural Changes in the Industrial Sector

Many structural changes have taken place in the industrial sector post-independence. The government has implemented number of policies for its development before 1990's. The Industrial policy has been considered "sine-qua-non" for speedy development of the country, irrespective of its developing status. However, it has got a special role to play in the overall development of country like India.

The measures to liberalize India's industrial policy framework begun in the late 1970s, which consisted of deregulation and de-licensing in certain industries, assigning a larger role to the private sector, and a gradual shift from direct physical controls to indirect controls (Raj, 1986[6]; Chandrasekhar, 1988[7]). The 1991- industrial policy reforms envisage the abolition of institutional entry barrier, viz., the system of industrial licensing, in all industries, except in a small list of strategic and potentially hazardous industries and in a few industries reserved for the small scale sector and the removal of investment controls on large industrial houses enforced under Monopoly and Restrictive Trade Practices (MRTP) act. Other measures under the reform package include the opening up of areas reserved for the public sector to the private sector and the decision to reduce the government share in public sector enterprises. Accordingly, the number of industries reserved for the public sector was reduced to six [1994] from seventeen [1991]. Alongside, many of the public sector enterprises were partially privatized, while retaining the government share in excess of 51 per cent. The licensing requirements for industrial investment were dispensed within all but eighteen industries. (See the detailed policy review in chapter II)

Policy changes in the external sector such as reduction in tariff and removal of non-tariff restrictions on imports, liberalization of the foreign investment and technology import policies and exchange rate policy reforms have a direct influence on the industrial sector. The licensing and other physical controls of imports were eliminated for non-consumer goods and tariff rates were drastically lowered. Import licensing was done away with for most goods, except consumer goods; import-weighted tariff declined to 27 per cent from (pre-1991) the level of 87 per cent; and exchange rates were devalued by 20 per cent (Ahluwalia and Little 1998, pp.4-5)[8]. The scope of foreign direct investment was widened. Further, the 1990s also witnessed several reform measures in the financial sector of economy that also have a bearing on the performance of industrial sector. In general, these policy reforms can affect the industrial productivity through a variety of channels. These include (1) increased competitive pressure, (2) greater and cheaper access to better foreign technology and imported intermediate commodities, (3) removal of various constraints on input use, technology choices and investment decisions of industrial firms, (4) greater technological dynamism and (5) more realistic exchange rate and favorable economic conditions.

The reforms were aimed at making the industry more efficient and productive, technologically up-to-date and competitive; with the expectation that efficiency and productivity improvement, technological up-gradation and enhancement of competitiveness would enable Indian industry to achieve rapid growth. In brief, the objectives were to raise the efficiency in productivity and achieve significant growth in the economy. The success of reforms should be judged in terms of this yardstick.

The present study expects answers for a few broad set of questions. The domestic industries were protected with tariffs and Quantities Restrictions (QRs) [pre-1991]. The tariffs found reduced [post-1991] with the phasing out of the quantitative restrictions.. We can identify from the figure1.2.[9]

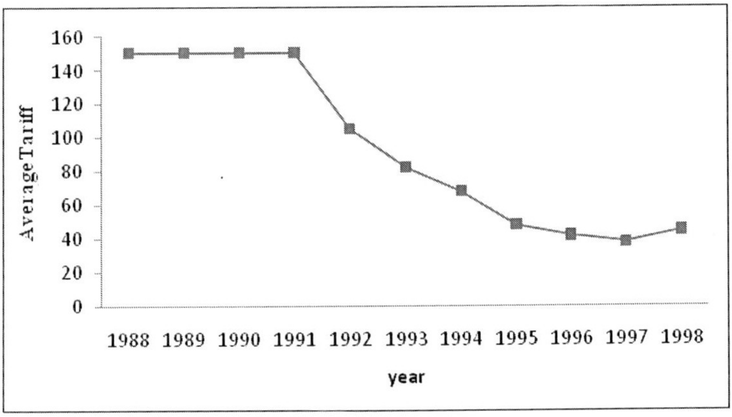

Source: Hasan, Mitra and Ramaswamy (2007)

Figure 1.2: Average Nominal Rate of Protection

According to Rajesh Mehta, the impact of Indian trade policy reforms on external trade"[10], the liberalization process has yielded to significant decline in the protection of domestic industry. Many riders were involved, viz., is there any impact on domestic industries from the Economic Openness? Is there any effective growth and efficiency from the said reforms? The issues ought to be addressed theoretically.

A number of studies have been examined to ascertain the impact of components of economic reforms on industrial performance. Most of them find the trade reforms in developing countries to have yielded growth in productivity, advancement in technology with resource reshuffle towards efficient firms, although some cases have failed to convince the hurdles involved in such methodology. This is true in the case of India, where some case studies have yielded to counterproductive results on slightly different methodologies. Aside methodological issues, India seems to be an exception with respect to trade liberalization of developing countries, and the 1991 Trade reform has resulted in reduced productivity.

The post-independence development strategy converged on national self-sufficiency, with the government regulating the overall economy. The latter half of decade 1980s, has shifted towards an export-led growth, supported by measures to promote exports at the cost of import liberalization. The theory appears to suggest anything could trigger productivity growth, after opening up to trade; the question has largely become an empirical one. However, until recently, the hypotheses linking trade with competition and productivity growth received relatively little empirical attention. Against this background, the present study gives detailed review literature that establishes economic openness and industrial performance (efficiency).

The Total Factor Productivity [TFP] factor:

Ahluwalia analyzed mixed trends in TFP and Partial Factor Productivities [PFP] in the domestic organized manufacturing sector ['59-'60 to '85-'86]. The TFP was measured for the 63 industrial groups based on the trans-log production function framework. To prepare the annual estimates, the annual data on value added, capital stock, employment, wages are being taken for organized manufacturing sector [Annual Survey of Industries –ASI]. The TFP growth was -0.4 per cent per annum, suggesting virtually zero growth the study period. There was a strong rising trend in capital-intensity, a weaker rising trend in labour productivity, and a secular decline in capital productivity[11].

Ravi kiran investigated on "Productivity in Indian manufacturing industries". Here, productivity indices as well as the growth rates of inputs (labour and capital) and output (Value Added) were analyzed between ['73-'74 to '95-'96]. The performance of domestic manufacturing sector in terms of TFP and PFP finds improved post-1981. The sectors involved were water works and supply, gas and steam, chemical and chemical Products, cold storage, transport equipment and parts and non-metallic mineral products projecting some improvement in labour and capital productivity. Appreciable part of the sector yielded positive growth of capital productivity in the subsequent period of analysis.

Kishor Sharma investigated on the consequences of liberalization on structural changes of manufacturing industry in Nepal. His study examined on the output structure and trade orientation following liberalization? Will there be any impact on manufacturing productivity? Will spatial distribution of manufacturing activity change? The results indicate some optimism in structural change with trade orientation following the liberalization drive but least improvement in productivity growth and spatial distribution of the sector. The export intensity rose significantly, despite poor productivity of export-oriented industries, post-liberalization. The impact of liberalization on the overall productivity remained nominal. It declined pre-liberalization and this continued to be so post-liberalization. A marginal improvement was detected in the latter period where the rate of decline in productivity was controlled post-liberalization. There were no signs of improvement in the spatial distribution of industries and with the tendency to locate in relatively developed region(s) continued even post-liberalization[12].

R.N. Agarwal have attempted on Technical Efficiency and Productivity Growth in the Central Public Sector Enterprises in India during 1990s. The objective of the study is to analyze the technological change, technical efficiency and total productivity growth of 58 large

Central Public Sector Enterprises (CPSE) ['90-'91 to '98-'99], group-wise and firm-wise. The partial productivities and the slow index of TFP have been used for estimating productivity growth at the industry group level, while panel data estimation method used the Random Effects Model and a modified form of Composite Error Term Frontier Production Function Model of Cornwell, Schmidt and Sickles, for estimating technological change and growth of technical efficiency at the firm level. The results show that the public sector enterprises haven't experienced any significant technological change during the decade 1990s. Further, the results indicate, decreasing returns to scale in production. They suggest a majority of the firms to have lower levels of technical efficiency with the efficiency remaining stationary. However, the growth of technical efficiency was apparent in some engineering firms.[13].

Anita Kumari examined on the productivity growth of domestic engineering industries pre and post- reform at the company level. The study is based on company level balanced panel data relating to domestic engineering industries, electrical and non-electrical groups, pre-reform ['85-'86 to '90-'91] and post-reform ['91-'92 to '94-'95]. The productivity growth of engineering industry declined post- reform, when compared to the pre-reform. The output growth had a significant positive impact on productivity growth, while the foreign equity participation had significant negative relationship with productivity growth in either period. The intermediate inputs imports had a strong positive effect on productivity growth post reform.

Mahadevan estimated the TFP growth 'using the South Korean manufacturing industry data for food, textile, chemicals and fabricated metal using the stochastic frontier approach ['80-'94]. The output growth was increasingly productivity-driven. The export-oriented industry experienced higher TFP growth. In the light industry like food and textile, technical efficiency change was negative, but in the heavy industry, i.e., chemical and fabricated metal, it was positive.

Sanja S., Pattnayak, Thangavelu, S.M. investigated the impact of economic reforms on the Indian domestic manufacturing industries using the panel data. A trans-log cost function is being used to analyze the production structure in terms of biased technical change and economies of scale. The panel had 121 manufacturing industries in service between ['82 to '98]. The results show the economies of scale (only moderate) in the domestic manufacturers in harnessing the key 1991 economic reforms. Most of the industries gave into bias technology change and capital-using technical change. The TFP value showed appreciable improvement post 1991 reform initiatives[14].

Euler Pereira G., R. Macedo estimated the TFP for 27 Brazilian domestic industries for the period 1996-2000. The annual growth was negative for almost three quarters of the analyzed sectors. The first period showed the growth of 2.9 per cent, whereas the second an average negative value of 8.1 per cent. The technical change was the key for domestic mining and manufacturing for conditioning TFP ['96-'98].

Goldar investigated the TEP growth for Indian domestic manufacturing industry using the Translog index ['79-'80 to '90-'91, '91-'92 to '97-'98 and '91-'92 to '99-'00]. The estimate was based on the value-added function framework. There was a considerable fall in value ['91-'92 to '97-'98], when compared to that [1979-80 to 1990-91] and much lower at one per cent ['91-'92 to '97-'98]. The estimated average annual TFP growth [1991-92 to 1999-00] exceeded that ['91-'92 to '97-'98], but was lower ['79-'80 to '90-'91].

Kumar, Surender have attempted on the TFP growth in the unorganized domestic manufacturing industry across 15 major states ['78–'79 to '00–'01]. Data envelopment analysis was used to compute Malmquist TFP index and its components. The results registered somewhat positive growth in the country. Most of the states witnessed higher TFP post-1990s reforms than pre-reforms. The Decomposition of the Malmquist productivity index showed improvement in technical efficiency rather than the technical progress towards the observed acceleration in growth.

Nik Hashim and Basri examined the TFP growth of Malaysian domestic manufacturing sector using stochastic frontier approach with translog production function. The duo found that lower growth for some industries, say below unity or even negative for transport and food industries ['90-'00] The positive growth was noted in chemicals, textiles, rubber, petroleum and wood. Here the technical efficiency was a major contributor except for those industries in chemicals, paper and petroleum. Petroleum projected highest technological progress. A highest technical efficiency was apparent in electrical and electronics industry, while the least in food industry.

Anita Kumari analyzed the impact of economic liberalizations on pattern of sources of output growth of Indian domestic manufacturing industry from the demand side perspective. The analysis was based on Chenery's factor decomposition approach [input-output framework]. It decomposes the output growth into four sources, viz., domestic demand expansion, export expansion, import substitution and intermediate demand expansion due to change in input-output coefficient. The analysis was done separately for the pre- and post-liberalization ['83-'84 to '89-'90, and '89-'90 to '97-'98], to examine the changing pattern in the sources of output growth as a result of policy liberalisation and structural reforms. The output growth was domestic demand driven with increased export pre and post-liberalization, but post-liberalisation, the contribution of domestic demand and export expansion has increased.

Metin Karadag, A. Ozlem Onders and Ertugrul Deliktas examined on TFP changes in Turkish domestic manufacturing industry. The private and public sectors were shortlisted in selected provinces of Turkey using panel data ['90-'98], through Data Envelopment Analysis (DEA) to compute Malmquist productivity indices, decomposed into two component measures, viz., efficiency change and technical change for the purpose of study. There was not much significant improvement for the time under consideration due to the instable economy in 1990s. Although there was small improvement, the results yielded efficiency change to have played a major role in TFP growth for the gestation period. The results also indicated any significant difference between public and private sectors. At the provincial level, among the total 18 provinces in Turkey, only six provinces showed deterioration cumulatively as far public sector was concerned. Amongst the improved provinces, three projected above five per cent, while cumulatively there was 6.7 per cent for all the provinces in private sector. Either sector in many provinces owed to efficiency change.

Nancy Y. C. Kong and Jose Tongzon examined the TFP growth in ten major sectors of Singapore. TFPG was estimated ['85-00] using the Malmquist Productivity Index-DEA method. The efficiency change was dominant in the retail sector, whereas technical change was dominant in the manufacturing sector. The former played a great part in TFP growth in the retail sector, upon the improvement in quality service of human capital that translated to efficiency of human organization in production capabilities. The catering sector was the worst performer using measures of efficiency, technical and TFP change.

Rajesh raj S N & Mihir K. Mahapatra have examined the performance of domestic organized industrial sector in some selected states ['81-'03] post-reforms. PFP and TFPM [Growth Accounting Method] were employed. The analysis revealed the performance of industrial sector to have witnessed noticeable change during the reforms. There has been substantial fall in the share of employment, Gross Value Added and Capital stock of the organized segment in the industrial sector as a whole during the reforms, implying an improvement in the share of unorganized sector in the said variables [1990s and onward]. Further, the growth of gross value added in selected states has declined during the reforms, as compared to the pre-reforms period, implying industrial sector to have failed to sustain the growth momentum in output [post-1991]. In this aspect, the performance of the state of Karnataka was somewhat better in comparison to other states, while the state of Orissa suffered the serious setback. Analysis of factor productivity growth reflects erosion in the organized manufacturing units with wider fluctuation in the reforms period, especially during the second generation reforms.

I.K.M. Mokhtarul Wadud investigated the productivity growth in Malaysian domestic manufacturing [1983-99]. Malmquist productivity Indices (MPIs) were computed using non- parametric Data Envelopment Analysis (DEA). Majority of industries operated at lower levels of technical efficiency with little or any improvement over time. Growth estimates revealed two-thirds of them (76 out of total 114 categories) experienced average annual productivity improvement ranging from 0.1 to 7.8 per cent. 95 industrial categories showed average annual technical progress while 53 industries showed technical efficiency improvement. The yearly average was relatively low from mid-1990 either there was decline in efficiency or technical regress. The results - glass and glass products (7.3 per cent), petroleum and coal (7.2 per cent), industrial chemicals (4.9 per cent) in respect of efficiency improvement and technical progress ranging between 0.8 per cent and 5.4 per cent and between 1.7 per cent and 4.1 per cent, respectively.

Kiran and Kaur have examined the impact of reforms on productivity level of Punjab manufacturing industries [1980-81 to 2002-03], for 16 manufacturing industrial groups. The results projected a fall in the capital and labour productivity post-reforms. The growth of value added and labour has witnessed a deceleration, while the growth in capital was positive. Of the 16 industrial groups 11 have witnessed higher TFP [pre-reforms] and five have higher TFP [post-reforms].

Saba Vahid has attempted on the productivity changes of the US domestic manufacturing sector. The productivity changed for the wood products ['97-'02]. The Malmquist Productivity Index (MPI) was selected to measure the productivity changes and Data Envelopment Analysis (DEA), a non-parametric approach, was used to measure the distance functions required for calculating the MPI. The results showed five per cent increase in productivity of the whole sector on average over the study period, while that of the wood product decreased by one per cent. The efficiency decline of the industry was the main contributor for the decline in productivity.

Atulan Guha has examined the structural change patterns in the domestic Indian organized manufacturing sector at the aggregated and the disaggregated three- digit level. The aggregate level grew at a faster rate pre-liberalized ['80s] than liberalized. The output and net value addition have shown higher growth ['80s]. The organized manufacturing sector grew at lower rate, the capital formation grew fast [liberalized]. The net fixed capital stock grew fast [liberalized]. The capital-intensity has also increased at a fast with negative employment growth [regime] declining the capital productivity. The capital has substituted labour instead of technological up-gradation. The organized manufacturing sector experienced a hike in the with the increase in the capital-intensity ['80s], showing technological up-gradation to have paid the dividend

The labour productivity increased in either periods, but the growth was higher in 80s. In the '80s, the increase in labour productivity depended on hike in capital intensity coupled with that of capital-productivity.

Abhay Gupta has analyzed the growth experience of registered domestic Indian manufacturing sector ['70-'03], using production function, index number and envelopment analysis methods. TFP growth rate average was 1.1 per cent for gross output-based and net value added-based measures. In gross output production, the share of materials was 0.6 per cent, much larger than the capital and labor shares. The share of capital increased constantly. The input growth jumped post-reform ('91-'97), but TFP growth was negative. The trend reversed [after '98], with slower output despite negative input growth due to larger TFP growth. The aggregated TFP growth rates (Domar-weighted and Fisher index) also followed similar pattern; showing upward trends after mid- 1990s. There were no significant differences in TFP growth rates among different-sized firms. After the reforms, the TFP growth increased substantially in the public sector corporations. The productivity transition seemed to be random across different (3-digit NIC code) industries. Industries with focus towards services experienced higher productivity growth than others. These results showed the lack of productivity growth was the reason for unimpressive performance of Indian domestic manufacturing earlier.

Jabir Ali, Surendra and E. Ekanem have attempted on efficiency and productivity changes in domestic Indian food processing industry. The study examined the performance of various segments of food processing industry in terms of TFP and efficiency change ['80-81 to '01-'02], using DEA approach. The domestic food processing industry grew at about 10 per cent per annum. The average technical efficiency score was estimated 0.902 under VRS model with average scale efficiency score of 0.870. This implies that the average technical inefficiency could be reduced by 10 per cent by improving scale efficiency and eliminating pure technical inefficiencies. The technical efficiency scores for food processing industry however declined [1990s in contrast with 1980s]. The returns to scale in food processing sector suggests that most of the sub-sectors have moved from increasing returns to scale towards constant and decreasing returns to scale during last two decades except meat and meat products, fish and fish products, fruits and vegetables as well as starch and starch products. An additional investment in the food processing segments yielded increased return to scale, encouraging profitable output and whereas food segments showed decrease or constant returns to scale, which needed reorientation and modernization in production. The food industry experienced positive change in TFP with varied magnitude across sub-sectors. The positive gain in TFP was basically due to change in technological progress i.e., shifted in the production frontier from increased doses of capital input.

Deb Kusum Das and Gunajit Kalita attempted to compute the aggregate productivity growth using the Domar aggregation technique. Building up from the Total Factor Productivity (TFP) growth estimates for 3-digit industries, they have used Domar weights to computed total factor productivity (TFP) growth for selected industries['80-'00]. The aggregate productivity for the selected 2-digit sectors showed sharp year-to-year fluctuations. The average TFP growth displayed wider differences for most of the 2-digit industries. The highest TFP growth went for leather products ['80-'85 and '91-'95], whereas chemicals enjoyed highest TFP ['86-'90]. The rubber and plastics industry similarly showed highest TFP growth ['96-'00]. Overall, they have found the productivity performance in the 1990s was poor in comparison with the 1980s, as evident for the number of industries registering positive TFP growth.

Sabuj Kumar Mandal, and S. Madheswaran examined the TFP growth in Indian domestic cement industry ['89-'90 and '06-'07] using company level data and applying Stochastic Frontier Approach. TFP growth was decomposed into technical progress (TP), technical efficiency change (TEC) and changes in scale component (SC). Empirical results showed the TFP growth was driven by SC and TP and not by TEC since TE was time-invariant in nature.

Shallu Sehgal and Suparn Sharma examined on the inter-temporal and inter-industry comparison of Total Factor Productivity (TFP) of the state of Haryana. Malmquist productivity index (MPI) model was used, which is an application of DEA to panel data to calculate the indices of TFP change, technology change, and efficiency change. The study was based on pooled data ['81-'82 and '07-'08] for different categories of organized sector manufacturing industries. The technical efficiency change was the key driver of TFPG in the manufacturing sector pre-reforms, however, the picture has turned around post-reforms. There was a positive impact of liberalization policy on technological advancement of the manufacturing sector. The state was inefficient post-reforms in the utilization of resources on hand and it was alarming about the incapability of the sector to cope up with the technological advancement.

Arnab K. Deb examined on the pre- and post-reform performances of Indian domestic manufacturing in terms of TFP growth ['70-'71 and '07-'08], to capture the productivity growth using the non-parametric method of Data Envelopment Analysis. The TFP growth was higher post-reforms at all-India level, though the majority of states experienced accelerated productivity growth, while some states experienced decline post-reforms. However, the regional variation in the rates of productivity change diminished post-reforms.

Fulwinder Pal Singh analyzed the TFP growth trends in Indian manufacturing sector at both aggregated and disaggregated inter-state levels. the Malmquist productivity index Used for panel dataset of 16 major industrial state over a period of 29 years spanning over 1979-80 to 2007-08, the study observed manufacturing sector of India is growing with 9.1 percent per annum growth of Total Factor Productivity (TFP) during the entire study period. Out of Sixteen Industrial states there are five states namely Uttar Pradesh, Madhya Pradesh, Gujarat, Orissa and Rajasthan where double digit TFP growth has been noticed. The manufacturing sector of Uttar Pradesh is growing with highest TFP growth at the rate of 12.8 percent per annum followed by Madhya Pradesh with TFP growth of 11.8 percent per annum. The analysis of the sources of the TFP growth in Indian manufacturing sector reveals that both technical progress and technical change are equally contributing TFP growth in sector under evaluation. It has also been observed that at all India level efficiency change is greater than technical progress.

S Ray examined the impact of liberalization on productivity growth of Indian domestic paper and pulp industry. Specifically, this study quantified the level of technical efficiency and technical change in this particular manufacturing sector. Malmquist Productivity Index method was used to different sub-sectors of the paper and pulp industry at aggregate level to examine the trend in productivity growth over a period of 28 years ('79-'80 to '06-'07]. There was decline in TFP growth post-reforms ('91-'92 and to '06-'07] showing adverse impact of liberalization at the aggregate level. The industry also experienced some regress in technological progress with stagnation in the technical efficiency. Non-responding technical efficiency change and the deteriorating technical change were the main ingredients responsible for declining productivity change in Indian paper industry and pulp industry.

Empirical Studies Related to the Inter-Relationship [Economic Openness and (Technical Efficiency) Industrial Performance]

Kalirajan and Zhao examined the impact of economic reforms on technical efficiency performance of China's state enterprises. The study used aggregated data at the provincial level for the manufacturing enterprises in the China ['86-'89] using Cobb-Douglas model. The coefficients were statistically significant level at five per cent. The mean technical constant increased from 78.6 to 84.8 per cent ['86-'89] The Technical efficiency of China's state enterprises from stochastic frontier production model was time-variant, suggesting some change in the level of technical efficiency across industries and periods across. There was a positive change and the technical efficiency increased in all the provinces of China during the study period. Clearly, the economic reforms [1980s] have had a positive and significant impact on improving technical efficiency of the state-owned manufacturing industries in all provinces of China.

Haishun Sun, Phillip Hone and Hristos Doucouliagos investigated the technical efficiency of industries in a transitional economy (China), using data for 28 manufacturing industries across 29 provinces with the Data Envelopment Analysis (DEA) approach. The technical efficiency of each industry was measured and compared across regions and provinces. There was considerable potential for savings in resource use in many industries. These savings were most apparent in the textile, timber processing and non-ferrous metal industries where, on average, output could be sustained at current levels, while at least halving the quantity of resources used. In general, the significant savings were indicated for most industries operating in the Central and Western regions of the country. An examination of the factors associated with differences in technical efficiency scores between industries found that there was generally positive relationship between export-orientation, foreign investment and technical efficiency in Chinese manufacturing industries. The Tobit regression analysis results confirmed export-orientation and foreign direct investment to have had a positive effect on technical efficiency. An inter-industrial comparison also indicated the industries whose products were highly oriented to international markets more technically efficient than domestic-market-oriented industries. The findings lend support to the hypothesis of a positive relationship between Economic Openness and Technical Efficiency.

Ephraim Wadonda Chirwa examined the level of technical efficiency in Malawian manufacturing industries using the deterministic (nonparametric) Data Envelopment Analysis Approach, used panel data for seven manufacturing industries ['84-'88]. Technical inefficiency was highest in most sectors. On average, firms in Malawian manufacturing sector producing existing levels of outputs, they could save inputs by 59 per cent in the tea industry, 44 per cent in the tobacco industry, 41 per cent in the wearing apparel industry, 62 per cent in the printing and publishing industry, 21 per cent in the soaps and cosmetics industry, 18 per cent in the plastic products industry and 13 per cent in the fabricated metal products industry. The results showed 15 per cent to have exhibited constant returns to scale, while 28 per cent and 56 per cent exhibited decreasing and increasing returns to scale, respectively. This shows that inefficiency was partly a result of operating at sub-optimal scale of production. The average annual efficiency scores for most sectors also showed a declining trend based on the 'inter temporal frontier approach', although this varies from industry to industry. There were decreasing trends in tea, tobacco and printing and publishing industries, while clearly visible increasing trends in wearing apparels and soaps and cosmetics. Average efficiency scores were more stable in plastic products and fabricated metal products industries.

The second empirical part of the study attempted to identify sources of technical efficiency in the selected manufacturing industries using a censored regression model. The results showed the market share of the firm as positively associated with the level of technical efficiency reflecting the importance of economies of scale. The domestic monopoly power was negatively associated with the level of technical efficiency.

Aggarwal attempted on the inter-firm determinants of export performance in Indian domestic manufacturing in the late 1990s. The objective was to test two hypotheses: first, in a liberalized regime, Multi National Enterprises (MNE) affiliates performing distinctly better than local firms in the export markets and second, MNE affiliates have had greater comparative advantages in high-tech than in low- and medium-tech industries. Tobit model estimations was conducted on all the sample firms. However, the evidence of the better performance of MNEs was not strong enough to suggest that India is attracting efficiency-seeking outward-oriented FDI. Even firms with higher foreign equity stakes have not performed distinctly better than others. The results also showed high-tech industries failed to attract efficiency seeking FDI as had been expected. In medium-high tech sectors their performance was somewhat better. In low-tech industries, firms with high foreign stake were found to be better performers. Two important implications of the results were: one, it appears that the economy was not fully integrated with the global economy and that the existing industrial and technological capabilities needed the reorientation to attract efficiency seeking FDI; two, India's competitive advantages still lie in low-tech sectors. The results suggest that in technology-based sectors own technological capabilities of firms were crucial determinants of export performance of firms.

Ephraim W. Chirwa evaluated the impact of privatization on the technical efficiency of six privatized enterprises, there state-owned enterprises, and six private enterprises competing three oligopolistic manufacturing industries [privatization drive '84-'91], using panel data on 'Inter temporal Frontier' approach for panel data. The findings showed the privatization in Malawi is being associated with high mean technical efficiency in privatized enterprises and competing state-owned enterprises and private enterprises. This finds the competitive process as more important than privatization in increasing the technical efficiency of all enterprises competing in the same industries.

Unni Jeemol, N. Lalitha and U. Rani studied on the trends in growth and efficiency in the utilization of resources in Indian domestic manufacturing sector [pre- and post-economic reforms]. Further, they compare the growth and efficiency across scale of production, that is, in the organized and unorganized manufacturing sector of the economy. They undertook a comparative analysis with Gujarat, as it is one of the most industrially developed states with a clear emphasis in its policies towards the secondary sector. The study shows that the pattern of growth in Gujarat was similar, with the organized sector growing rapidly during the reforms period, and the unorganized sector doing so immediately before the reforms. The organized and unorganized sectors in Gujarat seemed doing better than the all-Indian average in terms of growth of value added. Gujarat had an exceptionally high growth of value added in the reforms period in both organized and unorganized sector. This growth was reflected mainly in the basic and intermediate goods industries in the organized sector. The growth in manufacturing sector in Gujarat was also more efficient than the average all Indian growth post-reforms.

M. Parameswaran examined the performance of firms in four selected industries, in terms of efficiency against the background of economic policy reforms. The Stochastic frontier production function and an associated inefficiency model are being used to measure the time varying firm specific technical efficiency. The results indicated that although, the change in the policy environment has had a positive effect on the technical efficiency in all except in one industry, the level of efficiency was lower post-reforms in all the industries considered. The decline in the level of technical efficiency happened in a context of higher technical progress, identified as the upward shift of the best practice technology in all industries. This indicates that majority of the firms failed to catch up with the shifting frontier technology, resulting in an increase in their inefficiency. The hypothesis that a more liberalized trade regime enables the firms to acquire foreign technological knowledge through their export, import of technology and raw material import and thereby enhance the production efficiency was also examined. In this respect, he found that firm's export activity, import of technology and raw materials are contributing to higher efficiency.

Ali Ugur explored the technical efficiency levels in the electrical and optical equipment industry in Irish domestic manufacturing sector, with a stochastic production frontier approach ['91-'99] using firm-level panel data. Battese and Coelli (1995) model determines about the causes of inefficiency simultaneously, rather than employing a two-step approach, whereby efficiency estimates were being obtained in the first step, regressed on a set of determinants. The technical efficiency levels have increased in two sectors, namely electronic valves and other electronic components and radio and television receivers, whereas the electric motors and generators and medical and surgical equipment industries have experienced a decline in the average technical efficiency levels['91-'99]. The investment intensity reduces technical inefficiency levels of firms in all of the sub sectors without any significant relationship between export intensity and the technical inefficiency levels of individual firms in all but one sector, namely television and radio receivers industry. Overall, the results showed investment intensity and labour quality to have played an important role in reducing technical inefficiency levels of the indigenous firms in the electrical and optical equipments industry in Irish domestic manufacturing sector.

E. Abdul Azeez attempted on the performance of Indian domestic manufacturing sector in terms of economic Capacity Utilization (CU) ['74-'98]. The CU is estimated employing a translog variable cost function, using an iterative version of the Zellner's Seemingly Unrelated Regression Estimation (SURE) technique. The analysis reveals that the conventional installed capacity utilization measures underestimate the true economic utilization levels. Further, the Indian domestic manufacturing sector experienced a cyclical pattern of economic capacity utilization during the study period. It has also identified three distinct phases of economic CU movements. While the phase-one ('74-'84) has marked relatively wide fluctuations, the phase-two ('85-'90), showed more or less a stable level of utilization. A mild-variant of fluctuations of the sort was witnessed in the first phase, seen to have resurfaced in the third phase ('91-'98). The major point emerged from the study was the significant role of supply side as well as demand side factors in affecting the level of economic capacity utilization. The impact of economic reforms was not significant though the policy changes may influence supply and demand side factors determining the level of economic capacity utilization.

Jad Chaaban, Vincent Requillart and Audrey Trevisiol investigated the technical efficiency of French Cheese industry ['85-'00], used a two-stage procedure to identify whether production characteristics such as technical efficiency and returns to scale affect takeovers. Using the original panel data on French cheese manufacturers, first they estimated firm-specific productive efficiency and scale economies using Data Envelopment Analysis. In the second stage, they evaluated a random effects log it model of the determinants of takeover in the French cheese industry ['85-'00]. They have found that technical efficiency is not a significant determinant of takeovers, while the nature of scale economies is. Firms with Decreasing Returns to Scale (i.e. an over-sized production capacity) face a higher risk of takeover. This suggests that French cheese manufacturers have sought to expand their milk processing capacities by acquiring large firms. This may have been an indirect consequence of the non-transferable milk quota regime. By acquiring a competitor, a firm could be seeking an increased access to a scarce input that is absolutely needed to increase its production. The firm-specific effects were found significant. This indicated that one needs to incorporate individual firm-specific effects when modeling the takeover probability of cheese firms.

Oleg Badunenko, Michael. F and A. Stephan analyzed determinants of technical efficiency of German domestic manufacturing firms using a panel of about 35,000 firms ['92-'04]. Initially, they obtained estimates of technical efficiency and performed later an Analysis of Covariance in a second step to investigate the determinants of the technical efficiency of firms. The results of the fixed effects approach for obtaining estimates of technical efficiency appear rather reasonable. The distribution of technical efficiency was symmetric and most of the firms were clustered close to mean value. The analysis revealed that industry effects explain the largest part, more than one-third of the model's explanatory power of technical efficiency variation. Firm size was the second most important factor that has a strong significant effect on technical efficiency. The location of a firm's headquarter was also an important factor that explains another 10 per cent of variation in technical efficiency. The explanatory power of firm characteristics such as R&D intensity, outsourcing activity and the legal form is relatively small. Quite surprisingly, they found a negative effect of R&D intensity on technical efficiency, although with a very low explanatory power. This result may particularly indicate a time lag between R&D spending and the resulting efficiency improvements.

Neil Dias Karunaratne examined the impact of micro-economic reforms on technical efficiency of Australian manufacturing. The technical efficiency scores estimated for Australian domestic manufacturing industries using a combined stochastic production-frontier inefficiency model that is free of simultaneity bias. The model parameters have estimated maximum likelihood techniques using a panel data set covering a cross-section of 8 industries spanning a time-series of 26 years ('69-'95). The empirical results shed light on how technical inefficiency in manufacturing has been whittled down by the microeconomic reform induced trade liberalization and technology diffusion processes. Generalized likelihood ratio tests rejected the null hypotheses that trade liberalization and technology transfer had no significant impact on the reduction of technical inefficiency. The reduction of effective rate of assistance and technical efficiency and technology proxies such as intra-industry trade and capital deepening were negatively correlated during the study period.

Musleh–ud Din, Ejaz Ghani, and Tariq Mahmood have examined the efficiency of the large-scale manufacturing sector of Pakistan using two competing techniques, i.e., the Stochastic Frontier Analysis, and the Data Envelopment Analysis for two periods ['95-'96 and '00-'01], for 101 industries at the 5-digit. The results on the basis of stochastic production frontier showed that there was some improvement in the efficiency of the large-scale manufacturing sector, though the magnitude of improvement remained small. The results were mixed at the disaggregated level; whereas the majority of industrial groups gained in terms of technical efficiency, some industries showed deterioration in the efficiency levels, including, for example, transport equipment, glass and glass products, other non-metallic mineral products, and other manufacturing. These findings were broadly supported by the Data Envelopment Analysis, lending a measure of robustness. Overall, the increase in technical efficiency might be attributed to economic reforms, initiated in the late 1980s, that were aimed at improving competition and creating a better business climate for domestic and foreign investors. The market-oriented reforms opened up markets for imports and foreign investment, deregulated markets, and reduced government ownership. The reforms resulted in an increased role of market forces in resource allocation which in turn helped improve the efficiency of most of the industrial sector.

Nizamettin B and Gokhan D (2008) examined the performance measurement of Turkish and Chinese domestic manufacturing firms. They have compared the relative efficiencies of manufacturing companies of China and Turkey, using weight restricted Data Envelopment Analysis (DEA). Weights of inputs and outputs were estimated by canonical correlation analysis. The mean efficiencies of the firms of the two countries were compared by t-test. the result of the study showed China as more efficient in converting the resources to outputs than Turkey, when current ratio, total assets/total debt, inventory turnover, cash flow, receivable turnover, property plant and equipment/ total asset, number of employees were used as the resources and net income per employee, net income per share, earnings before interest and taxes margin and growth in sales as outputs for firms.

Suwanee A. and Gavind C Reid attempted on the technical efficiency of Thai domestic manufacturing sector. The main focus was on the relationship between varieties of capital investment and technical efficiency has been examined, based on the Battese and Coelli (1995) model. Estimates were obtained of the output elasticity of capital and the output elasticity of labour. Two explanatory variables, the addition to capital investment in land and the addition to capital investment in machinery and equipment, were found to have significant but different impacts on efficiency. On the one hand, the positive value of the coefficient for additional investment in land suggested the higher were such investments, the greater were inefficiencies (i.e., the lower were efficiency levels). On the other hand, the negative value of the coefficient of additional investment in machinery and equipment suggests that such investments improve the efficiency of the manufacturers. These results supported the view that post-crisis efficiency had improved partly, because of the increase in productive capital mobilized by the post crisis financial market restructuring, as well as because of the reduction in domestic interest rates. This suggests that, pre-crisis, the Thai manufacturing sector had suffered from insufficient productive capital investment, but this condition abated in the aftermath of the crisis, leading to signs of improvements in efficiency in the immediate post-crisis period.

The empirical findings of the performance of Indian manufacturing sector show mixed results. Many studies conclude that there was a decline in the TFP growth and technical efficiency in India post-reforms. The use of appropriate measurement techniques is very important in understanding the industrial performance, thereby suggesting better policy implications for Indian domestic manufacturing sector. Hence, various available measurement techniques were discussed in assessing the TFP growth and technical efficiency.

In the Indian context, many studies have focused on the domestic manufacturing industry, but based on technology classification, less attention was being paid in this field. The study was carried out on Economic Openness on industrial efficiency (productivity) based on the technology classification in transition period with using Data envelopment analysis.

Analytical Framework:

It is well known fact that the protection distorts resource allocation by attracting resources away from productive sectors towards the rent-seeking and directly unproductive activities. This results in the lower level of output and welfare than what could have been achieved in the absence of protection as shown in Figure1.3.[15] A'B' in the above figure is the production possibility curve of a country which shows the maximum limit of commodities X (exportable product) and Y (import substitution product) that can be produced in the absence of protection, supposing that this nation enjoys a comparative advantage in commodity X.

In the absence of protection, the relative commodity price would be determined at P, which determines the optimum level of production. At this point, the resources are efficiently utilized and the welfare is maximized.[16] Now, assume that tariffs and QRs are imposed on the imports of commodity Y and the tariff inclusive price is P*. Since, commodity Y is protected from external competition; it attracts

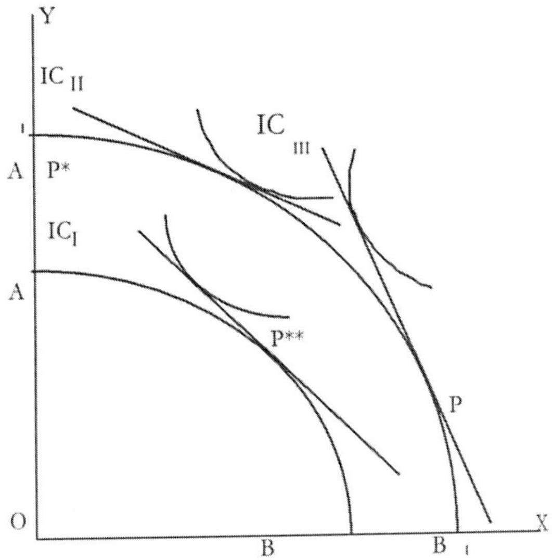

Figure 1.3: Effects of Protection on Production and Resource Allocation.

resources away from commodity X (exportable sector), leading to a fall in exportable output which is typically a labor intensive sector in developing countries. The decline in exportable output (commodity X) on the one hand, and the higher prices for the locally produced import substitution goods (commodity Y) on the other hand, result in the lower level of welfare as the nation now consumes at a lower indifference curve (i.e., IC_{II}). Frequently the more significant cost of protection is seen because of the loss of potential output either due to rent seeking behavior to receive preferential treatment or to the negative incentive effects which induce x-inefficiency. "These effects can push the production possibility curve inward from A'B' to AB, leading to a further decline in welfare as the nation now consumes at the lowest indifference curve (i.e., IC_{I}). The Protection also reduces efficiency by shielding domestic market from external competition and restricting access to imported inputs and technologies"[17]. However, Rodrik (1993) argues that there are no reasons to believe that protection discourages productivity improvement[18]. In fact, it is import liberalization, according to him that retards productivity growth by shrinking the domestic firm's sales and reducing incentives to invest in technological effort. Thus, whether liberalization really improves efficiency in Least Developed Countries (LDCs) or developing countries is ambiguous and must be examined empirically. In this connection objectives chosen for the study are given below:

Objectives of the Study

The study broadly aims at examining the Impact of Economic Openness on Industrial efficiency on Indian Industries Growth. More specifically, the objectives are:

[a] to review the Indian Industrial Policies, pre and post-transition.

[b] to analyze the trends in output growth (Value Added) and inputs growth (Labour and Capital) of selected Indian Manufacturing Industries (based on Technology Classification) pre and post-transition [aggregate and disaggregate level].

[c] to analyze the trends in productivity growth of selected Indian domestic manufacturing industries (based on Technology Classification) pre and post-transition [aggregate and disaggregate level].

[d] to examine the source of TFP of the selected Indian domestic manufacturing industries pre and post-transition..

Hypothesis

Ho: Economic Openness affected (In transition period) on industrial productivity growth, adversely

H_1: Economic Openness have made industrial productivity growth Efficacy, progressively.

Methodology

Area of the Study

Industrial activities in the country are broadly divided into factory and non-factory Sector. The factory sector covers units registered under Factories Act of 1948. Household and non-household industrial units not so registered constitute non-factory sector. The former is designated as registered or organized sector, the latter as unregistered and unorganized sector. All factories that employ more than ten workers with the aid of power and more than twenty workers without the aid of power are classified under registered manufacturing (or, broadly, the factory sector). All other manufacturing activities were classified are classified under unregistered manufacturing.

India largest and official industrial database, Annual Survey of Industries (ASI) covers the information about the registered manufacturing activities and does not cover the unorganized or unregistered manufacturing sector. The entire manufacturing activities in India are classified into 171 three-digit industries, which are again brought into 17 *two digit* industries. Using ASI data, this study analyses the performance and efficiency of registered manufacturing industry based on technology classification in India.

Selection of the Industries

In the era of globalizing world economy, the competitiveness of nations depend crucially on the speed of acquiring, absorbing and effectively utilizing new technology vis-à-vis their global competitors. Technology in the form of creative application of changes in technical knowledge results in productivity improvements. In the process, it provides the nation competitive advantage by infusing technical improvements in production process. Indian Science and Technology Policy (ISTP)-2001 clearly recognized the role of technology; aims to encourage in highest level of innovation and research and development in industry. In this connection the entire Indian manufacturing industries divided based on technological classification (which is developed by the Organization for Economic Co-operation and Development (OECD)[19] into four categories.

High Technology Industries

Medium High Technology Industries

Medium Low Technology Industries and

Low Technology Industries.

The detailed classification has given in the table 1.1. For this study, it has been consider and prepared the data based on the concordance between ISIC REV.2 CODE, NIC 87 CODE, NIC 98 CODE, NIC 2004, and 2008.

Table: 1.1 Concordance Table between ISIC REV. 2 CODE, NIC 87 CODE, NIC 98 CODE, NIC 2004, and 2008

Sr. No	*Industries*	*ISIC Rev.2 code Division / Major Group/Group*	*NIC 87 CODE*	*NIC 98 CODE*	*NIC 2004 CODE*	*NIC 2008 CODE*
	High – Technology Industries					
1	**Aircraft	3845	377	3530	3530	3030
2	Office and computing equipment	3825	(358+367)+394	3000+NA*	30	2620
3	Drugs and Medicines	3522	304	2423	2423	21
4	Radio ,TV and communication equipment	3832	(365+396)+366+368	(3220)+3230+3210	32	2630+2640+ 2610
	Medium-High-Technology Industries					
5	Professional goods	385	380+381+382	3311+3320+3330	33	2651+2652+ 2660+2670
6	Motor vehicles	3843	373+374+398	3410+3420+3430	34	29
7	Electrical machines excl.comm. equipment	383-3832	(360+395)+364+ (361+362+369)	(3110+3120)+NA+ (3130+3140+3190)	31	2710+2720+ 2790
8	Chemical excl. drugs (Industrial chemicals)	351+352-3522	(30+317)-305	(24)-2424	24 - (2424+2423)	20
9	Other Transport	3842+3844+3849	(371+372+397)+ (375+376)+(378+379)	(3520)+(3591+3592)+ (3599)	3520+3591+ 3592+3599	3020+ 3091+3092+ 3099
10	Non-electrical machinery	382-3825	(35)-358(390+391 +392+393)	(2813+29)-3000 (NA)	29	28
	Medium-Low-Technology Industries					
11	Rubber and plastic products	355+356	310+(311+312)+313	2511+1920+2519+ 2520	25	22
12	Shipbuilding and repairing	3841	370	3511+3512	3511+3512	3011+ 3012
13	Other manufacturing	39	(383+384)+385+386 + (387+388+389)	(3691)+3693+3692+ 3694+NA+3699	36	32

14	Non-ferrous metals	372	333+334+335+336 +337+338+339	2720	2720	2420
15	Non- metallic products	36	32	26	26	15
16	Metallic products	381	34	2811+2812+289	28	25
17	Petroleum refineries and coal products	353+354	(314+315) + (316+318+319)	2320+2310	23	19
18	Ferrous metals (Iron& steel)	371	330+331+332	2710	27-2720	24-(2420+2432)
	Low-Technology Industries					
19	Paper, paper products and printing	34	28	21+22	21+22	17+18
20	Textiles, apparel and leather	32	(23+24+25) +(26)+(29)	(171)+(172+173+181)+ 182+19	17+19+18	13+14+ 15
21	Food, beverages and tobacco	31	(20+21)+22	(15)+16	15+16	10+11 +12
22	Wood products and furniture	33	27	20+361	20+3610	16+3100

Source: *Classification* ***Based on*** *Organization for Economic Co-operation and Development (OECD) Science, Technology and Industry Scoreboard, 2003.*
*Note: *NA indicates not available of data **Air Craft exclude from the study due to lack of data*
ISIC: International Standard Industrial Classification, NIC: National Industrial classification.

Period of the Study

In this study, an attempt has been made to analyze the impact of economic openness on industrial efficiency. Since 1991, Indian economy has been constantly undergoing drastic economic reforms. Due to these reforms, so many changes have been taken place. Hence to capture these changes, have chosen the year 1991 is break point. The entire study divided into two vital periods and they are *pre* (1981-90) and *post transition period* (1991-2012) which is tested through structural break points.[20] (refer figure 1.4).

Data Sources

The current study is emphasizes empirical analysis of the data relating to the particular period from 1981-2012. And, for this purpose we have used the data collected from the Annual Survey of Industries, (ASI) compiled by Central Statistical Organization (CSO), Ministry of Statistics and Programmed Implementation. In India, ASI is the principal source of industrial statistics and has been compiled since 1959 under the authority of the Collection of Statistics Act, 1953. It provides statistical information to assess and evaluate, objectively and

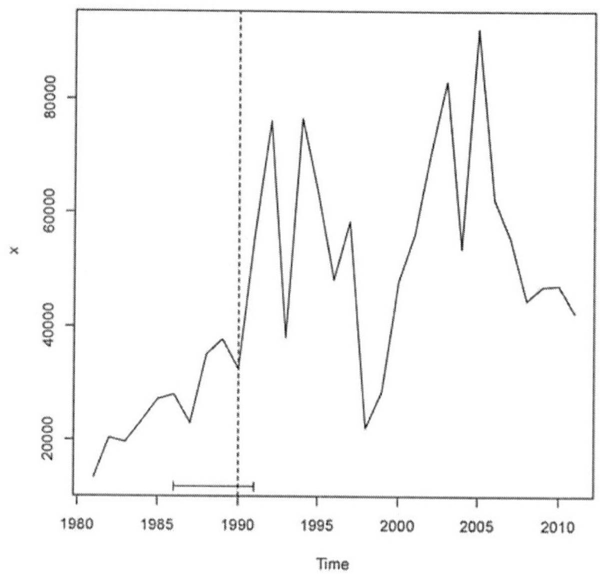

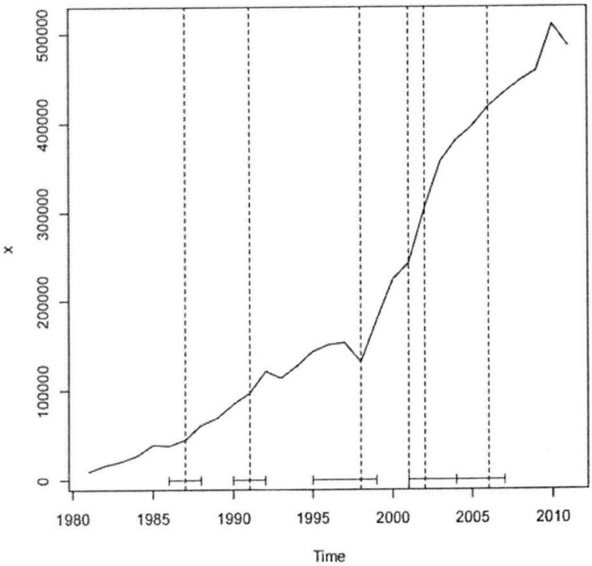

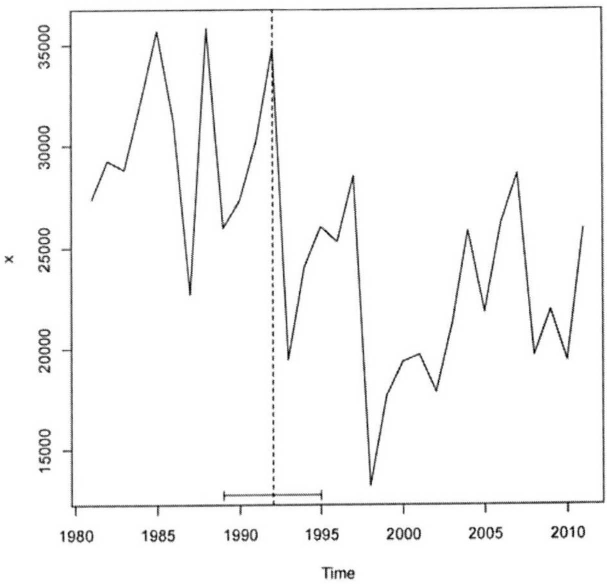

Figure 1.4: Structural break points of Indian Manufacturing Sector.

realistically, the changes in the growth, composition and structure of organized manufacturing sector. ASI covers all factories registered under Sections 2m (i) and 2m(ii) of the Factories Act, 1948, i.e., the factories employing or have employed 10 or more workers on any day of the preceding 12 months and in any part in which a 'manufacturing process' is being carried on with the aid of power; and those employing or have employed 20 or more workers on any day of the preceding 12 months and in any part of which a 'manufacturing process' is being carried on without the aid of power and does not include a mine, subject to the operation of the Mines Act, 1952.

The 'manufacturing process' referred above has been defined (vide Section 2(k) in the Factories Act, 1948 as:

Any process for making, altering, ornamenting, finishing, packing, oiling, washing, cleaning, breaking up, demolishing or otherwise treating or adapting any article or substance with a view to its use, sale, transport, delivery or disposal; or,

Pumping oil water or sewage; or,

Composing types for printing by letter press, lithography, photogravure or other similar process or book binding; or,

Constructing, reconstructing, repairing, refitting, finishing or breaking up ships or vessels.

Along with the above ASI data source we have used the Handbook of Industrial Policy and Statistics (Ministry of Commerce and Industry, Govt. of India), Hand Book of Statistics on Indian Economy (RBI), and Center for Monitoring Indian Economy (CMIE) issues. Descriptive analysis is based upon books, working papers and eminent expert's contributions to the trade and industries. And also reference to standard journals related to the trade and industries was made which are furnished in the bibliography.

Variables

In this study variables are used output, labour, capital. The definition of the variables and the deflators used are as given below:

(a) Output (GVA): In this study Gross Value Added used to represent output. GVA in this context implies increment to the value of output that is contributed by the unit, and is obtained by deducting the value of total inputs from the value of output. Use of Gross Value Added at constant prices to represent output is a common practice in the Indian empirical literature (Goldar, 1986; Ahluwalia, 1991; Balakrishnan and Pushpangadan, 1994; Balakrishnan and Pushpangadan, 1998).

The issue of using a suitable deflator for estimating the value added for series of price changes has been debated extensively (Balakrishnan and Pushpangadan, 1994; Ahluwalia, 1994; Dholakia and Dholakia, 1994; Goldar, 2002). Normally, the single deflator method has been used. In this method, the nominal value added is deflated by an index of the price of gross output (Goldar, 1986; Ahluwalia, 1991). However In this study, the Wholesale Price Index (WPI) for manufactured products has been used to deflate the nominal values of gross value added. The WPI, 1981-82 and 1993-94 has been arithmetically brought to a common base year (1993-94) through splicing method. For the present study, 1993-94 was chosen as base year.

Labour (LA): The Total number of persons engaged was taken as the measure of labo7ur input. As both workers, working proprietors and supervisory/managerial staff can affect productivity, so number of persons engaged is preferred to number of workers.

Capital (FC): Gross fixed capital stock at constant (1993-94) prices is taken as a measure of capital input. ASI provides data on fixed capital stock at historical cost. It consists of land, buildings, plant and machinery, capital work in progress, furniture, fixtures and office equipments and others. For constructing the capital stock for the sector, CSO's data on fixed capital stock for 1981-82 has been considered as the benchmark year of capital stock. The Capital stock series is then constructed by using perpetual inventory accumulation method. Most of the studies in the Indian manufacturing sector have used the Perpetual Inventory Accumulation Method (PIAM) to construct capital stock series (Ahluwalia, 1991; Balakrishnan and Pushpangadhan, 1994; Trivedi, 2004). This study also used the PIAM for generating the series on capital stock.

Capital stock for the industrial sector in the subsequent years has been arrived at by adding the real investment figures to the stock of capital of the previous year. The relationship between gross fixed capital stock in year t, denoted by K_t, the benchmark capital stock, K_0, the benchmark year for the present study is the year 1881-82 as the study covers the period 1981-82 to 2011-2012. Following Benerji (1975) and Balakrishnan & Pushpangadan (1994) double of the fixed capital is taken as measure of capital stock for the benchmark period ($K_{0} = 2$ (B_t), where t= 1981-82).

The investment series, (I_t), may be written as:

$$K_t = K_0 + \sum_{t=1}^{T} I_t$$

The investment figures were obtained using the formula:

$$I_t = (B_t - B_{t-1} + D_t) / R_t$$

Where B = Book value of fixed capital in the year't'

B_{t-1} = Book value of fixed capital in the year (t-1)

D_t = Depreciation in the year't'

R_t = Price index for machinery and machine tools (base year 1993-94)

Data Analysis Techniques

DEA Analysis

To test hypotheses, Malmquist Productivity Index methods used to calculate Total Factor Productivity (TFP) of the Indian Manufacturing Sector based on technological classification. DEA based Malmquist productivity approach has been used extensively to measure performance in various sectors. Detail methodology has explained in the fifth chapter.

Organization of the Study

The present study can be divided into five chapters. First chapter deals with a brief introduction of Economic Openness, discussed on industrial structure before 90s, review of literature related to impact of Economic Openness on industries efficiency and productivity which has been already debated by various eminent economists, objectives of the study, methodology and sources of data. In the second chapter, reviewed evaluation of industrial reforms. Third chapter gives a vivid analysis the growth performance of Indian Manufacturing Sector (based on technological classification) during the pre and post transition periods for different industries as group-wise as well as individual industry. The growth rates of value added, capital stock and labour are estimated and evaluated of different periods. Chapter four discusses on the efficiency (productivity growth) of Indian manufacturing industry; using Malmquist Data Envelopment Analysis for selected industry groups for different periods. Finally, chapter five devotes to present the summary of study and findings and also draw major conclusions of the study. Based on the theoretical and empirical analysis, various policy suggestions are recommended for the better performance of Indian Manufacturing Sector as a whole in general and selected industries in particular.

References

1. Economic Openness comprises Liberalization, Privatization and Globalization [LPG].
2. Statement of the Union Finance Minister in Parliament on December 16, 1991.
3. Corbo, Vittorio & Fischer, Stanley, (1995), *"Structural adjustment, stabilization and policy reform: Domestic and international finance,"* Handbook of Development Economics, in Hollis Chenery & T.N. Srinivasan (ed.), Handbook of Development Economics, edition 1, volume 3, chapter 44, pp. 2845-2924.
4. Randolph, B. and Campos, N. (2010), *"The Growth Effect of Foreign Direct Investment in Low-Income Countries: A Meta-Regression Analysis of the Firm-Level Evidence,"* London, DFID Systematic Review Programme Report No. 1.

Note: Different researchers have tried to establish a possible link between Economic Openness (liberalization) and productivity .the process of liberalization would lead to more competition in an economy. This increase in competition would pressurize the firms to be technically efficient by increasing organizational competence, skills of the labour, capacity utilization and making the firms more innovative. This would probably result into more efficient use of resources. On the other hand, due to liberalization process i.e. second link establishes that would allow the firms to have international exchange of information, easy access to technology, imported inputs and access to global capital thereby, resulting into higher productivity gains and higher economic growth.

5. Aussilloux, V., Boumellassa, H., Emlinger, C. Fontagne, L. (2010), *"The economic consequences for the UK and the EU of completing the Single Market"*, BIS Economic Paper to be published in February 2011.

6. Raj, K.N. (1986), *New Economic Policy*, *Oxford University Press*, Delhi.

7. Chandrasekhar, C.P. (1988), *"Aspects of Growth and Structural Change in Indian Industry*", *EPW*, Special Number, Vol. 23, Nos. 45-47, November, pp. 2359-2370.

8. Ahluwalia, Isher Judge and Little, I. M. D. (1998), *" Introduction"* in Ahluwalia, Isher Judge and Little, I. M. D. (eds.) (1998), *India's Economic Reforms and Development: Essays for Manmohan Singh,* Oxford University Press, Delhi.

9. Hasan, R., D. Mitra, and K.V. Ramaswamy (2007), *"Trade Reforms, Labour Regulations, and Labour-Demand Elasticities: Empirical Evidence from India," Review of Economics and Statistics*, 89(3, August), pp. 466–81.

10. Rajesh Mehta (1997), *"Trade Policy Reforms, 1991-92 to 1995-96. Their Impact on External Trade",* ERPW XXXII No. 15, April 12, 1997.

11. Ahluwalia, I.J. (1991), *Productivity and Growth in Indian Manufacturing*, Oxford University Press, New Delhi.

12. Kishor Sharma (2000), "Liberalization and Structural Change: Evidence from Nepalese Manufacturing", *Discussion Paper* No. 812, Yale University and Charles Sturt University, Australia.

13. Agarwal, R.N. (2001b), *Technical efficiency and productivity growth in the central public sector enterprises in India during 1990s*, Discussion Paper 28/2001, Institute of Economic Growth, New Delhi.

14. Sanja S. Pattnayak, Thangavelu, S. M (2003), "Economic Reform and Productivity growth in Indian Manufacturing Industries An interaction of technical change and scale economies" *Working Paper* No. 0307, Department of Economics, National University of Singapore.

15. Kishor Sharma (2000*), "Liberalization and structural change: evidence from Nepalese manufacturing Economic Growth Centre"*, Yale University, Discussion Paper No. 812.

16. This is because by exchanging X for Y the nation ends up consuming at the highest indifference curve (i.e., ICIII)

17. Srinivasan, T.N. and J. Bhagwati (1999), *"Outward-orientation and Development: Are Revisionists Right?"*, Economic Growth Centre, Yale University, Discussion Paper No. 806.

18. Dani Rodrik, (1993), *"Trade and Industrial Policy reforms in Developing Countries: AReview of Recent theory and evidence"* National Bureau of Economoic research, Working paper No 4417,Camridge,Newyork.

19. OECD Science, *Technology and Industry Scoreboard*, 2003.

20. The foundation for estimating breaks in time series regression models was given by Bai (1994) and was extended to multiple breaks by Bai (1997ab) and Bai & Perron (1998). Breakpoints implements the algorithm described in Bai & Perron (2003) for simultaneous estimation of multiple breakpoints. The distribution function used for the confidence intervals for the breakpoints is given in Bai (1997b). The ideas behind this implementation are described in Zeileis et al. (2003).

Chapter - II

Evaluation of Industrial Policies

Introduction

After Independence, the Government of India spelt out its approach to the development of the industrial sector in the Industrial Policy Resolution 1948. The Industrial Policy Resolution, 1956; the Industries (Development and Regulation) Act, 1951, to regulate and control the development of private sector; and the MRTP Act [Monopolies and Restrictive Trade Practices Act] - 1969 was adopted to prevent concentration of economic power and control monopolies. Another legislation that had considerable implication for industrial policy (as far as the participation of foreign companies in domestic industrial sector is concerned) was the Foreign Exchange Regulation Act (FERA) adopted in 1973. However, the measures, which guided and determined the state intervention in the field of industrial development failed to achieve the objectives. They created a number of anomalies, distortions and rigidities in the system. The government went on liberalizing the industrial policy during 1970s and 1980s. The drastic approach was on in 1991 with the New Industrial Policy (NIP).

Circumstances during NIP

In the summer of 1991, India suffered worst B.O.P. since 1947. The position with the sector owed to the crisis in the latter half of 1980s. The inflow of foreign borrowal increased at fast pace due to the excess of domestic expenditure over income. The fiscal deficit of the

Centre and the State rose to 11 per cent ['91]. The political need to undertake large-scale maintenance import was financed by short-term barrowings. The total public debt as a proportion of GNP doubled up to 60 per cent. The foreign currency reserves were exhausted. Matters worsened by an accompanying double-digit inflation ['90-'91].

India's credit rating got reduced for the first time. It was on the edge of default on its international commitment; when denied access to external commercial credit market. A net outflow of Non Resident Indian (NRI) deposits commenced in October '90. The only way left for India was to borrow against the security of gold reserves transported abroad. Some good prospect emerged and from the '91 Balance of Payments, long overdue necessitated for the economic reforms (*Economic Openness*). Apart from macroeconomic stabilization, structural reforms were introduced in the industrial and trade policy regime for improved growth, efficiency, productivity and international competitiveness.

Industrial Policy Regime

The economic reforms were on in all the sectors of Indian economy. Major policies were framed for the Indian industrial sector. The Industrial policy document of 1991 states "the major objectives of the new industrial policy package will be, to build on the gains already made and correct the distortion or weakness that may have crept in, maintain a sustained growth in productivity and gainful employment to attain international competitiveness. The pursuit of these objectives will be tempered by the need to preserve the environment and ensure the efficient use of available resources. All sectors of industry whether small, medium or large, belonging to the public or private or cooperative sector will be encouraged to grow and improve on the past performance. The policy will be endeavored for continuity with change."[1]

In pursuit of the above objective, the government has decided to take a series of initiatives with respect to the policies undermentioned:

Industrial Licensing

Foreign Investment

Foreign Technology Agreement

Public Sector Policy

MRTP Act

Industrial Location Policy

Abolition of Phased Manufacturing Programme for new projects

Removal of Mandatory Convertibility Clause

Industrial Licensing

Industrial licensing is governed by the industries (Development and Regulation Act 1951). The industrial policy revaluation of 1956 identified the following three categories of industries: i) those reserved for development in the public sector, ii) those permitted for development through private enterprise with or without state participation, and iii) those where the investment initiatives would ordinarily emanate from private entrepreneurs.

The changing industrial scene in the country and the policy underwent several modifications. Industrial Licensing Policy and procedures were liberalized.

It was imperative to make a number of changes in the system of industrial approval. The major policies initiate to encourage domestic entrepreneurs by assisting them meet in emerging domestic and global challenges. The foundation of any such package of measures must be for entrepreneurs to decide on investment under discretion. Technological dynamism and international competitiveness requires enterprises respond swiftly to the fast changing external conditions that have become characteristic of the industrial world. The Government policy and procedures must be geared up to assist entrepreneurs in their efforts. This can be so, if the authorities extend help through fully transparent procedures.

Flexibility in the licensing policy calls for bold and imaginative decisions designed to remove restraints on capacity creation, ensuring that national interests are not jeopardized. The industrial licensing system swerved from the concept of capacity licensing. The system of reservation for public sector undertaking was on greater flexibility and the private sector could enter in these areas on a case-by-case basis.

As a sequel for economic liberalization, the new industrial policy abolished all procedures of industrial licensing, irrespective of the level of investment, except for certain industries related to security and strategy, social reasons, concerns of safety and overriding environmental issues, manufacture of unsafe products and articles of elitist consumption. However, of the 18 industries, three industries (motor cars, white goods and raw hides and skins and leather) were de-licensed [April '93]; entertainment electronics industry [December '96]; five industries (animal fats and oils, tanned or dressed fur skins, chamois leather, asbestos and asbestos – based products, plywood and other wood and paper and newsprint) [July '97]; four industries (coal and lignite, petroleum products, bulk drugs and sugar) – ['98-'99]. Now, five items of health strategy and security consideration remain under the purview of industrial licensing. Alcohol cigarettes, hazardous chemicals, electronics aerospace and defense equipment, and industrial explosives were under the purview. In respect of de-licensed industry, no approval is required from the government. However, entrepreneurs were required to submit an Industrial Entrepreneur Memorandum (IEM) to the Secretariat for Industrial Approvals (SIA) provided the investment value on plant and machinery exceed Rs.10 crore.

Foreign Investment

Foreign Direct Investment has played so far a minimal role. The current account deficit during 1980s was not large, in terms of external commercial borrowing, external assistance and non- resident bank deposit inflows.

The overall needs of funding contributed 21.8 per cent, 24 per cent, and 25.5 per cent, respectively. However, the adjustment programme ['90-'01], enabled an appreciable Foreign Direct Investment (FDI).

The Government attracted appreciable foreign investment to enhance the resources availability in infrastructure and critical areas of economy. "The rules have been considerably eased. The World Bank considers India's present foreign investment regime more liberal than those prevailing in Asean countries (including China, Indonesia, Taiwan and Thailand), in attracting foreign investment)"[2].

Under the global integration drive, the Government has been allowing the multinationals to enter the country not just with their products, but with direct finance, for participating in units with the latest technology. The options have led the government adopt more liberal measures:

The foreign competition in the domestic market is expected to stimulate local producers minimize production cost and offer improved products, services and

The economy will benefit from the inflow of modern technology accompanying foreign investment.

The new policy encourages foreign investment through,

Foreign Direct Investment (FDI), and

Foreign Institutional Investment (FII)

Foreign Direct Investment

FDI policy went liberalized ['91] to let automatic foreign Investment up to 51 per cent of equity in 34 priority sectors, which extended later to 48 sectors. The limit was up to 50 per cent, in the mining sectors, and up to 74 per cent in nine specified sectors[3] under the Non-resident Indian (NRIs) and oversea corporate bodies (OCBs). NRIs could hold at least 60 per cent of equity and invest up to 100 per cent through automatic route. No approval is required for FDI inflow up to 24 per cent of the equity in any Indian firm and up to 20 per cent in any new private bank (40 per cent for NRIs).

The investment limit for telecommunication services (basic, cellular and paying) is 49 per cent; domestic air taxi operation or airlines is 40 per cent (100 per cent for NRIs) and the bulk drugs producing pharmaceutical sector is 51 per cent. FDI ignored by automatic route include: the small scale sector; items requiring industrial license under existing policy; and items for aerospace and defense equipment, whether specifically mentioned or not; and other items relating to production and use of atomic energy. The limit was subsequently raised from 51 per cent to 74 per cent and on to 100 per cent for many industries. FDI is at present permitted up to 100 per cent on the automatic route in most of the sectors, subject to sectoral rules or regulations. FDI is prohibited in retail trading (except single brand product), atomic energy, lottery, gambling and betting.

Foreign Institutional Investment

Investment inflow by Foreign Institutional Investors (FIIs) and through Global Depository Receipts (GDRs) policies underwent drastic changes. The domestic companies were permitted to raise the capital through Euro-Market issues of Global Depository Receipts (GDRs) and Foreign Currency Convertible Bonds (FCCBs). The reputed FIIs include those heads viz., pension funds, mutual funds, asset management companies, investment trusts, nominee companies and incorporated or institutional portfolio managers, who could invest in the Indian capital market. The investors ought to be registered institutions within their respective home countries or those of origin, ought to revise with the guidelines of Securities and Exchange Board of India (SEBI). An FII can invest up to 10 per cent, while a group of FIIs up to 30 per cent of share capital of listed companies. The investment could go with non-listed companies, subject to the approval of limit by its Board of Directors with a special resolution passed by their general body. FIIs, as such, can hold up to 100 per cent of the equity in debt-funds, and government securities. The profits from portfolio investment could be repatriated freely, subject to Indian foreign exchange regulations.

Foreign Technology

Industrial environment needs to acquire the acquisition of technological capability receives priority. In the fast changing world of technology, the relationship between the supplies are between technology users, which must be a continuous process; and such relationship becomes difficult, when the approval process includes unnecessary governmental interference on a case-to-case basis, involving endemic delays, fostering uncertainty. The government is expected to provide automatic approval for technology agreement related to high priorities within the specified parameters, in its bid to inject the desired level of technological dynamism in the industry.

Similar facilities will be available for three industries. Such agreements seldom require any expenditure of free foreign exchange.

The domestic companies are free to negotiate with foreign counterparts, in terms of technology transfer under their discretion.

Public Sector Role

The new economic policy recognized the weaknesses and shortcomings of the public sector and its working and suggested for a re-look at the same. Action plan was initiated in five important aspects of the sector. The main idea was to withdraw as many industries from the sector as possible, leaving appreciable field open for the private sector. Accordingly, the areas reserved for the sector were to be reduced without allowing any new enterprises.

The new policy recognized the heavy financial burden by them on the exchequer. A new approach was suggested, which proposed for a realistic review, since it involved those areas where it is not expected to take off, In the words of the then Union Finance Minister, "it is in the national interest that public sector enterprises become more efficient, more productive and more profit-oriented".

The government often promised the sector to play the rightful role involving domestic socio-economic scenario, as envisaged in the Industrial Policy Resolution of 1956, with the anticipated innovation in the strategic areas of national importance.

The sector, as such, has not generated internal surplus on a large enough scale. It has contributed to a high–cost structure, because of inadequate exposure to competition;.

The government has decided to adopt a new approach, to address these problems, for which the key elements are,

(i) The existing portfolio of public investments shall be reviewed with a greater sense of realism to avoid areas, where social considerations are not paramount, or the private sector would be more efficient;

(ii) Enterprises in areas, where the continued public sector involvement was judged appropriate shall be provided a much greater degree of managerial autonomy.

(iii) The budgetary transfers for them will be progressively reduced.

(iv) Competition from private sector will be encouraged. Part of the equity in selected enterprises will be disinvested. They shall be brought under existing market discipline.

(v) Chronically sick enterprises will not be allowed to incur heavy losses.[3]

These points were re-emphasized in the government's subsequent memorandum to the IMF. "The key elements of the government's strategy for public enterprise reforms are strengthening the managerial autonomy; the promotion of increased private sector competition in areas, where social considerations are not paramount; reducing budgetary constraints and increasing the dividend payments to ensure an adequate return on the government equity; partial divestment of equity in selected enterprises to mobilize non-inflationary resources and widen public participation, in order to introduce a greater sense of accountability; and restricting or closure of patently unviable enterprises."[4]

There will be a review of the existing portfolio of public investments in respect of industries based on low technology. These include, small-scale and non-strategic areas [inefficient and un-productive, with least social consideration for public purposes], and such areas, where the private sector has developed sufficient expertise and resources. The focus in the public sector will be on strategic, hi-technology and essential infrastructure areas. Accordingly, the priority areas for their growth in future are:

Essential infrastructure – goods and services

Exploration - oil and mineral resources.

Crucial areas - Technology development and building of manufacturing capabilities, where the private sector investment is found inadequate,

Manufacturing of products, where strategic considerations predominate, such as defense equipment.

The areas reserved for public sector were reduced to six, where security and strategic concerns predominate. The government opened the arms and ammunition sector to the private sector [May 9, 2001].

The sector is being left with three industries, atomic energy, minerals specified in the schedule to the atomic energy and rail transport.

The policy talks of more operational freedom to managements through MOUs (Memorandum of Understanding). MoUs were being signed even in the past. No new measures were required, except to speed up the process. Accordingly, the number of public sector units (PSUs), which signed MoUs, went up to 110 [1996-97] as compared to 104 [1995-96]. There was no change was noticeable either in the relations between the PSUs and the Administration Ministries or in their overall performance.

The government proposed to devote special attention to those undertakings, which were sick and decided to refer them to the Board for Industrial and Financial reconstruction (BIFR). If we obverse the Economic survey:

> "that sickness is a serious problem in many public sector units; this government has amended the Sick Industrial Companies Act to bring public sector undertakings within its purview. This makes [sick public sector units] them subject to similar discipline as the private sector units, including those units referred to the Board for Industrial and Financial Reconstruction (BIFR), for identification of a viable restructuring package or closure, as the case may be"[5].

The chronically sick units, unlikely to be turned around, for the formulation of revival/ rehabilitation schemes, will be referred to the BIFR, or similar higher-level institutions created for the purpose. A social security mechanism will be created to protect the interests of workers, who are likely to be affected by such rehabilitation packages.

The Union Finance Minister clarified that:

> "This does not mean that all sick units will be closed down. All units, which are potentially viable units, will be provided opportunities and resources for restructuring. Only patently unenviable units will need to be closed down and that too after formulation of credible social safety nets to protect the interest of workers in the affected enterprises. Our efforts will continue to avail opportunities for gainful employment for those people, able and willing to work"[6].

Out of 246 PUSs, ninety eight were reported to be incurring losses (accumulated losses being opportunity Rs.10, 000 crore) and fifty eight were considered beyond the redemption. The total work force employed was of the order of 4.17 lakh workers. The accumulated losses stood as high as Rs.25, 000 crore. The government promised the budgetary supports to loss making Public Sector Enterprises (PSEs) in the form of 'non-plan' loans, and the enterprises will be phased out by 1994-95. This public enterprises survey (1996) mentioned about the following non-plan loans in the budgets Rs.779.33 Crore [1993-94]; Rs.901.47 crore [1994-95]; and Rs.1, 133.70 crore [1995-96]. The figure went up after the initial decision was taken to reduce the same.

The public sector equity was proposed to be disinvested up to 49 per cent in selected profit-making enterprises, not only to mobilize non-inflationary resources for the budget, but also to broad-based ownership for wider public participation. Mutual funds, financial institutions, general public and workers were made the targeted beneficiaries. It was anticipated that such move would facilitate their managements commercially viable, and induce them fall in line with the existing market discipline.

The enterprises were being allowed not only to form joint ventures, but also to mobilize equity afresh from the market to finance their expansion plans. In this way, the performance of an enterprise could be measured in terms of financial profitability from the capital market. The Boards of such companies would be made more professional and given greater powers, more flexibility in respect of any decision taken on pricing. A decision was taken with seriousness on the package of disinvestment. It was recommended by V.Krishnamurthy Committee and Dinu—Khatkhate Committee [1992] and C. Rangarajan Committee [1993]. However, the government failed to take their recommendations seriously.

Most of the countries, have created special high-level bodies to deal with the problems associated with effective disinvestment of public sector enterprises.. Perhaps, the G.V. Rama Krishna committee on disinvestment was established in August 1996, in response to the recommendation of *The India Infrastructure Report* (Rakesh Mohan

Committee, 1990). It called for the setting up of 'High-powered and expert institution for public sector restructuring'.

The commission has advised the government on the methodology, time, size and price of disinvestment of the public sector shades and was about to draw a long-term programme. The intention was to make the disinvestment exercise more transparent and responsive.

The government has announced about its intention to offer a part of government shareholding in the public sector enterprises to mutual funds, financial institution, the general public and the workers. A beginning in this direction was made [1991-92] by disinvesting part of the selected public sector equities [1991-92 to 2005-06]. The government has mobilized nearly Rs. 49,214 crore through these modes. The new industrial policy indicated the government's intention to invite a greater degree of participation by private sector in important areas of the economy.

Monopolies and Restrictive Trade Practices Act (MRTP)

The main objectives of the MRTP Act are as follows;

1. Prevention of concentration of economic power to the common detriment;
2. Control of monopolies
3. Prohibition of monopolistic trade practices;
4. Prohibition of restrictive trade practices
5. Prohibition of unfair trade practices.

The Act was designed to avoid economic concentration of the power in the Indian economy by exercising surveillance and adopting proper measure in case the economic concentration proves to the common detriment of general public. Concentration was measured in terms of the prescribed value of the assets owned or controlled by any undertaking, singly or along with interconnected undertakings or as a dominant undertaking. The objective that was sought to be achieved at that time through the MRTP Act was ensuring that large industrial houses, which were covered by the definition under section 20 of that Act97, in terms of the value of the assets they controlled, did not deprive smaller enterprises of their share of the resources of the country and that large industrial houses fell in line with the country s planning priority. The main purpose of the MRTP Act was, containment of concentration of economic power not issues relating to competition, through prohibition of monopolistic and restrictive trade practices restraining competition was also within the scope of the Act. The MRTP Act deals and regulates Trade practice.

Industrial location policy liberalized

An important item of the policy was related to the location of industries. The policy was made much more flexible, which follows:

"In location other than cities of more than one million population, there will be no requirement of obtaining industrial approvals from the central government, except for industries subject to compulsory licensing. In respect of cites with population greater than one million, industries other than those of a non-polluting nature such as electronic, computer software and printing will be located outside 25km of the periphery, except in prior designated industrial areas. A flexible location policy would be adopted in respect of require industrial regenerations. However, the zoning, land-use regulation and environmental legislation under the jurisdiction of local authorities will continue to regulate industrial location"[7].

Abolition of Phased-Manufacturing Programmers [new projects]

To force the pace of indigenization in manufacturing, phased manufacturing programmers have been in force in a number of engineering and electronic industries. The new industrial policy has abolished such programmers in facture as the government feels that due to substantial reforms made in the trade policy and the devaluation of the rupee, these are no longer any need for enforcing the local content requirement on a case-by case, phased manufacturing programmers will continue.

Removal of mandatory convertibility clause

A large part of industrial investment in India was financed by loans from banks and financial institution. These institutions have followed a mandatory practice of including a convertibility clause in their lending operations for new project. This has provided them an option of converting part of their loans into equity, if felt necessary by their management. Although, this option has not generally been exercised, it has often been interpreted as an unwarranted threat to private firms of takeover by financial institutions. The new industrial policy envisaged the financial institutions will not henceforth impose this mandatory convertibility clause.

Appraisal of New Industrial Policy

According to J.C. Sandesara "the new industrial policy seeks to raise efficiency and accelerate industrial production in five different ways"[8].

They are as follows:

A number of changes in industrial licensing policy, foreign investment, foreign technology agreement and MRTP Act are such as to do away with the prior clearance of the government. In such cases, the project time and project cost will be reduced. Material and human resources engaged in cultivating contacts and 'getting things done' will be released for more productive uses. Thus efficiency will be improved.

The changes in respect of foreign investment and foreign technology agreement are also designed to attract capital, technology and managerial expertise from abroad. This will raise the availability of such scarce resources in the country on the one hand, and will improve the level of efficiency of production on the other hand.

Some changes as regards public sector may enhance the 'allocative efficiency'. Opening up of eleven areas (so far reserved for the public sector) to the private sector implies an opening for the sector which, by and large, has given a better account of itself.

Other measures in this area, such as the purposeful formulation and implementation of Memorandum of Understanding [MoU] and its monitoring, professionalization, greater autonomy may be expected to improve the performance of the enterprises that will remain the public sector.

Greater emphasis will be made in controlling and regulating monopolistic, restrictive and unfair trade practices and the strengthening of the powers of the MRTP Commission will curb the anti-competitive behavior of firms in the monopolistic, oligopolistic and ineffectively competitive markets and thus promote competition and efficiency.

Boosting Manufacturing Sector [Other major policies]

National Manufacturing Policy (NMP)

The government has taken a number of initiatives to improve the industrial climate and boosting the domestic manufacturing sector. "The Government of India notified the National Manufacturing Policy [November 04, 2011] with the objective of enhancing the share of manufacturing in GDP to 25 per cent within a decade and creating 100 million jobs. It also seeks to empower the rural youth by imparting necessary skill sets to make them employable. Sustainable development is integral to the policy and the technological value addition in manufacturing has received special focus. The policy is based on the principle of industrial growth in partnership with States. The Central Government will create the enabling policy frame work, provide incentives for infrastructure development on a Public Private Partnership (PPP) basis through appropriate financing instruments, and the State Governments will be encouraged to adopt the instrumentalities provided in the policy. One of the instruments in the NMP is the creation of National Investment and Manufacturing Zones (NIMZ) as planned Integrated Industrial Townships. Nine NIMZs have been announced, eight of which are along the Delhi Mumbai Industrial Corridor (DMIC)"[9].

"Major feature of NMP is the rationalization and simplification of regulations based on the basic principle of self-regulation of industry to the extent possible. The Central/State Governments will suspend the operation of particular provisions, wherever such powers exist subject to an alternative mechanism, annual audits by concerned departments and third party certification. For the effective implementation of the NMP, a number of institutional structures have been constituted. These include Manufacturing Industry Promotion Board (MIPB), under the chairmanship of Minister for Commerce and

Industry Minister; High Level Committee (HLC) under the chairmanship of Secretary, DIPP; Board of Approval (BOA) under the concerned Joint Secretary. A 'Green Manufacturing Committee (GMC)' has also been set up, to promote the green-technology for manufacturing [environment friendly] under NIMZ"[10].

Ministries engaged in manufacturing sector [Implementing policies, programme, and Schemes]

There are number of Ministries/ Departments which implement various policies, programme, schemes that contribute to growth of manufacturing. These include Ministry/ Departments of Micro Small & Medium Enterprises, Heavy Industries, Steel, Textiles, Food Processing Industries, Chemical & Petro Chemicals, Fertilizers, Pharmaceuticals, Petroleum & Natural Gas, Defence Production, Electronic & IT, Shipping etc. On an estimate, about 30 schemes relating to manufacturing are being implemented by these Ministries/ Depts. Efforts are on to discuss with these Ministries/ Departments, feasible measures to reverse the current slow down on manufacturing and achieve the goals of the NMP. Efforts are also on to build data banks of schemes/ programmes, training institutes / agencies, R&D and centers of excellence to provide a common knowledge platform and enable sharing of common facilities/ resources/ inputs.

MSMEs play a crucial role in driving growth of manufacturing sector, export and creating employment. The traditional labor-intensive sectors like textiles, leather, manufactures, handicrafts and carpets have huge potential. Manufacturing sector needs a boost with special emphasis given to MSMEs. Besides NIMZ, SEZs are key tools for facilitating the growth in the Manufacturing Sector.

References

1. Industrial policy document 1991, Government of India.
2. *"India: Recent Economic Developments and Prospects"*, A World Bank country study, Washington DC 1995, p. 43.
3. *"Memorandum to IMF"*, December 1991, p. 13.
4. *"Memorandum to IMF"*, July 1992, pp. 5-6.
5. *"Economic survey"*, 1991-92, part 1, government of India.

6. Dr.Manmohan Singh, Finance Minister, Government of India, Recent Developments in India Economy, Part I edited by Uma Kapila, Academic, Foundation, 1992.
7. Reserve Bank of India, *Report on currency and finance*1998-99, p. 8.
8. J.C Sandesara, "New Industrial Policy: Questions of Efficient Growth and Social objectives," Economic and Political Weekly. August 3-10, 1991, page no. 1870.
9. Jitender Singh, (2013), *"Analysis of Trends in the Manufacturing Growth in Last Five years"*, *Research Studies* ,Office of the Economic Adviser, Department of Industrial Policy &Promotion, Ministry of Commerce & Industry, Government of India.

10 *Ibid.*

Chapter - III

Growth Performance Analysis

[Domestic Industries under Technological Classification]

Introduction

Developing countries have been progressively adopting market-friendly reforms [1980s and 1990s]. Indian economy underwent similar reforms. Changes took place in the almost all the important sectors of Indian economy due to reforms (*Economic Openness*), The performance of domestic industries underwent noticeable changes post-Independence. There has been a diversification of the industrial sector with variation in growth. The growth [pre-1950s to mid-1960s] was substantial, with deceleration [mid-1960s to post-1970s], revival [1970s] leading to appreciable level [1980s]. A series of economic reforms were introduced on the macro-economic scale to revitalize the economy, wherein certain industrial and trade policy reforms found their way.

The industrial sector reforms were to enhance its efficiency and growth. The impact of reforms on its growth needs to be examined. The debate has revolved around the performance of domestic manufacturing Sector post 1991 era. It remained controversial and attracted many researchers.

Whether the shift in policy regime has made any significant changes [post-1991]?

The study, as such, commences with an examination of the growth performance of domestic manufacturing sector.

In this chapter, an attempt is being made to examine the growth performance of the manufacturing sector based on technology classification.

High Technology [HT],

Medium High Technology [MHT],

Low Technology [LT]

and Medium Low Technology Industrial Sectors [MLTI]

The analysis was carried out between 1981-82 and 2011-12.

To analyse impact of the Economic Openness on Indian Industries and the entire study period has been broadly divided into two - pre-transition period (1981-91) and post- transition period (1991-2012).

To study the growth performance of these industries, variables used in the analysis are the Gross Value Added (GVA), Fixed Capital (FC) and Labour (LA).

In order to observe the performance of industries growth, rates were computed according to the following formula:

$$P_t = P_o (1 + r)^n$$
$$P_t / P_o = (1 + r)^n$$
$$1 + r = (P_t / P_o)^{1/n}$$
$$r = (P_t / P_o)^{1/n} - 1$$

where P_t = current year value

P_o = initial year value

r = compound annual growth rate

n =number of years

The study gets divided into two sections.

Section I deals with macro-level growth performance analysis.

Section II provides an analysis of the impact of Economic Openness on industrial growth w.r.t. particular group of industries based on technology.

Growth Performance Analysis at Macro-level

Indian Manufacturing Sector in Pre-transition Era

Three important phases of the industrial growth can be identified.

These are the *first phase* [1950-51 to 1964-65], *second phase* [1965-66 to 1970s] and *third phase* [1979-80 to 1989-90]. The first phase was the phase of rapid industrial growth. The manufacturing sector grew at an average rate of 5.8 per cent in the early half of fifties and 6.5 per cent in the latter half of the decade. The growth was mainly due to the second five year plan for strong capital base through public sector investment, in the light of emergence of private sector.

The second phase reflected the deceleration of industrial growth. The late sixties and seventies witnessed the emergence of macro political-economic uncertainties, such as the wars with Pakistan and China, rising prices, oil prices shocks, licensing requirements for investment, reservation of industries in the public sector.

The third phase revived the growth with the gradual withdrawal of constraints and controls through sequential policy reforms.

Table 4.1 below shows the growth rates in manufacturing sector [1950-51 and 1989-90]. The 1980s showed some improvement.

Table 3.1: Growth of Domestic Manufacturing sector [Pre-transition]

Sectors	*1950-51 to 1955-56*	*1956-57 to 1965-66*	*1966-67 to 1979-80*	*1981-82 to 1989-90*
Manufacturing	5.8	6.5	4.3	5.8
Registered	6.2	8.2	4.5	7.6
Unregistered	5.6	4.5	4.1	3.4
GDP	3.6	3.6	3.4	5.6

Source: Central Statistical Organization

Paradigm Shift of Industrial Policy

[Manufacturing Sector in Post-Transition]

The Industrial Policy since 1991 has been facilitating the development. The industrial licensing was abolished for most of the industries, There were only five industries related to security, strategic and environmental concern, where an industrial license was required. The reforms were initiated in areas of reservation of products for exclusive production in the small scale sector. The government has also enacted the Micro, Small and Medium Enterprises Development (MSMED) Act, 2006. The investment ceiling has been stepped up for Rs.5 core [small enterprises], and Rs. 10 core [medium enterprises].

Table 4.2 indicates manufacturing growth at an average 7 per cent [1992-01] which was up to 7.4 per cent [2001-12].

Table 3.2: Indian Manufacturing Sector [Post-Transition]

Sectors	*1992-93 to 2000-01*	*2001-02 to 2011-12*
Manufacturing	7	7.4
Registered	7.4	9.1
Unregistered	6.4	5.7
GDP	6.2	7.5

Source: Central Statistical Organization

Trends in Employment and GDP

Table 3.3 shows that the sectoral share of employment.

Compiled from various NSSO rounds- 1987-88 onwards to 2009-10.]

There has been about 13 percentage point reduction in the employment share in agriculture despiste no such increase in the manufacturing share. In fact, there has been a decrease in the share of employment [2004-05 and 2009-10]. Table 3.4, showed the decline of number of persons employed in manufacturing from 56 mn [2004-05] to 52 mn [2009-10]. Some 4 million workers were withdrawn from the sector. Sluggish global demand for major export items like textiles, handicrafts, leather made the managements to axe the workers.

Table 3.3: Sectors Share in Employment

NSSO Rounds	*Reference Years*	*Agriculture*	*Manufacturing*	*Industry*	*Services*
66th	(2009-10)	51.8	11.4	21.9	26.3
61st	(2004-05)	56.5	12.2	18.7	24.8
55th	(1999-00)	60.1	11	16.3	23.6
50th	(1993-94)	64.3	10.5	14.8	20.9
43rd	(1987-88)	64.5	11.2	16.1	19.4

Source: Computed from various rounds of NSSO

Table 3.4: Manufacturing Sector -Number of Persons Employed [in mn]

NSSO Rounds	*Reference Years*	*Rural*	*Urban*	*Total*
66th	(2009-10)	24.12	28.23	52.35
61st	(2004-05)	27.76	28.3	56.06
55th	(1999-00)	22.99	21.99	44.98
50th	(1993-94)	19.55	17.9	37.45
43rd	(1987-88)	19.73	19.16	38.88
38th	1983	15.84	14.65	30.49

Source: Computed from various rounds of NSSO

International level comparison [GDP and Employment];

Table 3.5 gives a clear picture about the share of domestic manufacturing sector added value added in GDP and share of industrial employment in total employment across a few countries. The Manufacturing value added of GDP is 14 per cent in India compared to 13 per cent in United States and 31 per cent in China. The share of employment in industry is total of 22 per cent in India as compared to 27 per cent in China. The Table as follows:

Table 3.5: Share of Indian Manufacturing Sector in GDP and Employment in Industry

Countries	*Manufacturing Value Added (% of GDP)*	*Employment in Industry (%) of total employment)*
Thailand	36	20
China	31	27
Korea	31	17

(Cont'd...)

Malaysia	26	27
Japan	19	25
Sri Lanka	17	25
Brazil	15	22
Pakistan	15	20
India	14	22
US	13	17
Indonesia	11	19
Bangladesh	10	15

Source: World Bank Note: Figures are ranging from 2009-2011

Trends in Export of Indian Manufacturing Sector

Manufacturing production and exports have been driving the rapid growth of many dynamic emerging economics. Table 3.6 and figure 3.1 gives a clear picture about the trends in exports of domestic manufacturing sector between {1981-82 and 2012-13]. There has been a sharp acceleration in India manufacturing exports performance from mid 1990s (post transition period) when compare to 1980s (pre transition period). During the last decade of reforms, India's exports have performed well. Positive policy measures combined with robust

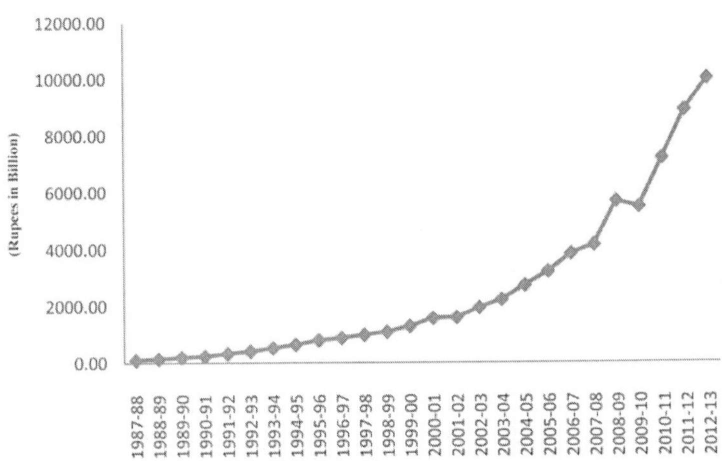

Figure 3.1: Exports of Manufactured Goods

growth of world trade have led to this improved performance. Compared to pre-liberalization period, India's export to GDP ratio has increased. And also The Table 3.7 shows that the Sector wise Exports of Indian Manufactured products performance. Almost all sectors (Textile and Textile Products, Manufacture of Leather, Chemicals and Related Products, Manufacture of Metals, Machinery and Instruments, Pharmaceuticals & others, Transport Equipment, Electronic Goods and Petroleum Products) steady rise from 1990s.

Table 3.6: Exports of Manufactured Goods

Year	*Manufactured Goods*
1987-88	106.26
1988-89	146.41
1989-90	199.32
1990-91	233.19
1991-92	324.13
1992-93	406.6
1993-94	522.45
1994-95	640.67
1995-96	794.33
1996-97	873.77
1997-98	986.6
1998-99	1085.06
1999-00	1287.61
2000-01	1568.58
2001-02	1591.46
2002-03	1947.65
2003-04	2228.29
2004-05	2728.72
2005-06	3212.61
2006-07	3842.61
2007-08	4145.99
2008-09	5664.02
2009-10	5464.56
2010-11	7198.63
2011-12	8885.99
2012-13	9996.12

Source: Directorate General of Commercial Intelligence and Statistics.

Table 3.7: Sector-wise Exports of Manufactured Products (Rupees in Bn)

Year/ Products	*Textile and Textile Products*	*Manufacture of Leather*	*Chemicals and Related Products*	*Manufacture of Metals*	*Machinery and Instruments*	*Pharmaceuticals & others*	*Transport Equipment*	*Electronic Goods*	*Petroleum Products*	*Other Manufactured Goods*
1987-88	39.08	12.51	10.26	2.88	5.15	6.86	2.53	2.00	6.49	1.08
1988-89	43.99	15.22	15.79	4.42	7.38	11.20	3.63	2.90	5.05	1.32
1989-90	62.38	19.50	25.87	7.42	10.05	18.79	5.26	5.04	6.97	1.64
1990-91	77.92	26.00	31.01	8.19	12.49	22.16	7.19	4.17	9.38	1.40
1991-92	115.69	31.28	46.07	11.94	14.33	34.53	12.24	6.54	10.22	2.09
1992-93	145.03	37.00	51.73	16.22	15.69	33.25	15.46	6.15	13.79	4.04
1993-94	171.64	40.76	74.56	20.80	20.04	43.07	18.57	9.52	12.48	4.87
1994-95	223.49	50.57	96.30	22.17	22.82	55.35	24.22	12.94	13.09	6.74
1995-96	268.65	58.61	120.32	27.64	27.76	72.56	30.94	22.42	15.18	8.91
1996-97	306.57	57.01	138.90	32.43	37.53	88.66	34.39	27.82	17.10	9.51
1997-98	336.36	61.57	163.39	38.03	44.44	104.87	34.53	28.23	13.11	8.76
1998-99	373.01	69.87	168.67	43.75	48.59	111.68	32.05	21.15	3.76	9.63
1999-00	425.62	68.91	203.95	53.11	51.27	133.82	35.11	29.51	1.69	11.82
2000-01	515.55	88.83	268.89	72.08	72.19	167.39	45.31	48.04	85.42	16.26
2001-02	486.77	91.10	288.62	76.50	82.70	176.32	48.69	55.86	101.07	18.52
2002-03	562.21	89.45	360.80	89.42	97.20	225.45	64.55	60.63	124.69	23.02
2003-04	587.79	99.39	434.06	111.50	127.58	268.62	89.88	79.42	163.97	28.18
2004-05	609.06	108.81	559.11	152.83	167.12	320.77	127.14	82.31	314.04	36.96
2005-06	726.18	119.44	653.90	187.42	224.80	404.09	191.39	96.21	515.33	43.55
2006-07	786.13	136.50	784.42	229.92	304.20	495.88	223.98	129.14	845.20	54.89
2007-08	782.09	141.01	853.28	283.89	367.50	561.73	282.82	135.32	1141.92	52.52
2008-09	920.62	163.55	1044.42	347.17	503.42	718.80	512.98	313.01	1233.98	61.02
2009-10	941.89	159.46	1086.87	262.03	452.56	748.06	466.10	258.95	1328.99	74.27
2010-11	1103.75	178.18	1315.44	385.28	539.42	879.59	731.21	373.78	1887.79	96.45
2011-12	1343.12	229.72	1778.16	459.19	685.82	1175.48	1013.11	424.19	2679.15	122.07
2012-13	1487.73	264.99	2172.57	545.97	827.88	1471.43	1001.65	438.83	3276.79	143.08

Source: Directorate General of Commercial Intelligence and Statistics,

Note: Due to change in commodity classification by DGCI&S, data on'from 1970-71 to 1975-1976 and 1976-77 to 1986-8 may not comparable.

Growth Performance Analysis of Technology Based Classification

Growth Rates of Gross Value Added, Capital and Labour in High Technology Manufacturing Sector

The trend rates of growth of GVA provide in the Table 3.8 stood at 10.3 per cent for aggregate High Technology Manufacturing Sector of the entire study period. In terms of Gross Value Added the Radio, TV & Communication Industry is the best performer with a growth rate of 13.2 per cent and followed by Office & Computing Equipment Industry. On the contrary, the worst performing industry was Drug & Medicines with 8.6 per cent rate of growth.

A further analysis of pre and post transition period suggests that the trend in growth rate of GVA during post transition period had increased from 6.2 per cent to 13.6 per cent for the entire High Technology Manufacturing Sector. Almost all industries are positive in the post transition period. The highest growth rate of GVA recorded by Radio, TV & Communication Industry was 21.2 per cent and the lowest growth rate of GVA recorded by Drug & Medicines Industry indicates 10.2 per cent.

It has been noticed that the growth rate of capital recorded 17.2 per cent for aggregate High Technology Industrial sector of the entire study period. The growth rate of capital was attained the highest 20.7 per cent in the Office & Computing equipment Industry during the entire study period. The Drug & Medicines Industry was the lowest 15.4 per cent in growth rate of capital of this period.

A pre and post transition period comparison analysis depicts that the trend in growth rate of capital during post transition period have increased from 13.6 per cent to 21.8 per cent for the entire High Technology Manufacturing Sector. Almost all industries are in positive growth rate of capital recorded in the post transition period. The growth rate of capital is highest in the Office & Computing equipment Industry to the extent of 32.0 per cent and the lowest growth rate of capital was recorded by the Drug & Medicines industry to the extent of 16.3 per cent in the post transition period when compare to pre transition period.

At the aggregate level, the growth rate of labour was found lower than the Gross Value Added and Capital in all the industries during the entire study period. In most of the industries, the growth rate was found to be less than 2 per cent during this period. A further analysis of pre and post transition period suggests that the trend in growth rate of labour during post transition period was negative and it was fallen from 3.9 per cent to -1.67 per cent for High Technology Manufacturing Sector at aggregate level. The highest growth rate of labour was found in the Office & Computing equipment industry to the extent of 3.0 in the post transition period. Drug & Medicines Industry has scored the lowest growth rate of labour to the extent of -3.9 during this period.

However, at disaggregate industrial level of pre and post transition period comparison depicts that the trend in growth rate of labour during post transition period have been decreased drastically in almost all industries.

Table 3.8: Compound Annual Growth Rates (CAGR) of High Technology Manufacturing Sector Pre and Post Transition Period

Industry Group	*Value Added*			*Capital*			*Labour*		
	Pre Transition period	*Post Transition period*	*Entire period*	*Pre Transition period*	*Post Transition period*	*Entire period*	*Pre Transition period*	*Post Transition period*	*Entire period*
Office& Computing Equipment	7.5	11.9	11.3	12.5	32.0	20.7	-0.0	3.0	-1.4
Drug &Medicines	6.0	10.2	8.6	14.4	16.3	15.4	2.0	-3.9	3.5
Radio, TV & Communication	6.2	21.2	13.2	13.5	27.6	19.2	8.4	1.3	2.7
Aggregate	6.2	13.6	10.3	13.6	21.8	17.2	3.9	-1.67	2.8

Source: Computed using the data from Annual Survey of Industries, EPW Research Foundation.

Growth Rates of Gross Value Added, Capital and Labour in Medium High Technology Manufacturing Sector

The Table 3.9 depicts a synoptic view of the trend in growth rate of GVA of Medium High Technology Manufacturing Sector at aggregate and disaggregates level. The pattern of growth of GVA in the Medium High Technology Manufacturing Sector stands at 7.1 per cent for the entire study period. Industry-wise calculated growth rates reveals that Professional goods Industry and also Other Transport Industry recorded the highest growth rate of 12.5 per cent during the entire study period in terms of GVA and followed by Chemicals excl. drugs industry with 7.9 per cent. The lowest growth rate of GVA recorded in the Electrical machines excl.com equipment Industry with 4.1 per cent.

A comparative analysis of pre & post transition period shows that there has been an increase in the growth rate of GVA at aggregate level from 6.8 per cent in pre Transition period to 8.7 per cent in post transition period in the Medium High Technology Manufacturing Sector. Out of 6 industrial groups, 5 industries have witnessed acceleration in the growth rate of GVA during the post transition period. The highest growth rate of GVA was found in the Other Transport Industry with 14.8 per cent in the post transition period. Non electrical industry has lowest growth rate of GVA with 5.8 per cent during the same period.

It has been noticed that the growth rate of capital was recorded as 13.1 per cent for aggregate Medium High Technology Manufacturing Sector in the entire study period. The growth rate of capital is highest with 17.1 per cent in the Professional goods industry and the lowest was recorded in the Electrical machines excl.com equipment industry with 11.6 per cent in the same period. A pre and post transition period comparison depicts that the trend in growth rate of capital during post transition period it was decreased from 17.6 per cent to 10.2 per cent for the entire Medium High Technology Sector. Almost all industries are witnessed turn down in the growth rate of capital recorded in the post transition period. The growth rate of capital highest in the Professional goods industry to the extent of 27.4 per cent and lowest growth rate of capital recorded by Non-electrical industry to the extent of 16.6 per cent in the pre Transition period when compare to post transition period.

Table 3.9: Compound Annual Growth Rates (CAGR) of Medium - High Technology Manufacturing Sector Pre & Post Transition Period

Industry Group	*Value Added*			*Capital*			*Labour*		
	Pre Transition period	*Post Transition period*	*Entire period*	*Pre Transition period*	*Post Transition period*	*Entire period*	*Pre Transition period*	*Post Transition period*	*Entire period*
Professional goods	11.8	12.9	12.5	27.4	10.7	17.1	2.7	2.2	2.3
Motor vehicles	8.9	6.4	7.3	17.8	14.0	15.4	6.2	-0.7	2.3
Electrical machines excl.com equipment	1.9	8.9	4.1	16.9	8.4	11.6	1.6	-3.6	-1.2
Chemicals excl. drugs	7.0	10.5	7.9	17.3	10.0	12.8	0.9	1.5	1.2
Other transport	12.9	14.8	12.5	20.3	9.5	14.1	6.5	1.5	3.1
Non-electrical	4.9	5.8	5.0	16.6	8.9	12.0	0.7	-1.4	-0.5
Aggregate	6.8	8.7	7.1	17.6	10.2	13.1	2.2	-0.4	0.7

Source: Computed using the data from Annual Survey of Industries, EPW Research Foundation.

Growth rate of labour is lower than the value added and capital in all the industries during the entire study period at the aggregate level. In most of the industries, the growth rate was found to be less than two per cent during the same period. A Pre and Post transition period comparison analysis suggests that the trend in growth rate of labour during post transition period has negative from 2.2 per cent to -0.4 per cent for Medium High Technology Manufacturing Sector at aggregate level. Out of 6 industrial groups, 3 industries have witnessed acceleration in the growth rate of labour during the pre transition period except others such as Professional goods, Chemicals excl. Drugs and Other transport Industries. And, whereas the Electrical machines excl.com equipment, Non- electrical and Motor vehicles Industries recorded negative growth rate of labour during the Post transition period.

Growth Rates of Gross Value Added, Capital and Labour in Low Technology Manufacturing Sector

The Table 3.10 illustrates that the growth pattern of GVA in Low Technology Manufacturing Sector. The total GVA recorded an overall growth of 7.7 per cent for the entire Low Technology Manufacturing Sector. The Industry-wise analysis reveals Food, beverages and Tobacco Industry recorded the highest growth rate of 6.0 per cent and the lowest GVA was found in Wood products and furniture with 3.4 per cent in the same period.

A comparative analysis of Pre & Post transition period reveals that an average growth rates of GVA was same at aggregate level of Low Technology Manufacturing Sector. And another point is to understand in this period was that almost all industries growth rate of GVA decreased in Post transition period compare to pre Transition period. The highest growth rate of GVA was found in the Food, beverages and Tobacco Industry to the extent of 9.8 in the pre Transition period and followed by Textiles apparel and Leather Industry with a growth rate of 7.0 per cent. Wood products and furniture Industry was found at the lowest growth rate of 1.8 per cent in the post transition period.

The pattern of growth of capital in the Low Technology Manufacturing Sector stands at 13.3 per cent for the entire study period.

Table 3.10: Compound Annual Growth Rates (CAGR) of Low Technology Manufacturing Sector Pre & Post Transition Period

Industry Group	*Value Added*			*Capital*			*Labour*		
	Pre Transition period	*Post Transition period*	*Entire period*	*Pre Transition period*	*Post Transition period*	*Entire period*	*Pre Transition period*	*Post Transition period*	*Entire period*
Paper, paper products and printing	4.6	3.8	3.8	15.6	9.3	11.8	-0.2	-0.2	-0.1
Textiles, apparel and leather	7.0	3.3	4.2	17.8	10.9	13.7	-1.9	1.0	0.2
Food, beverages and tobacco	9.8	3.7	6.0	18.5	10.2	13.6	-1.8	0.6	-0.4
Wood products and furniture	6.2	1.8	3.4	17.2	13.0	14.2	-0.4	0.8	-0.3
Aggregate	8.7	8.6	7.7	17.5	10.3	13.3	1.4	0.6	0.9

Source: Computed using the data from Annual Survey of Industries, EPW Research Foundation.

Industry-wise calculated growth rate reveals that Wood products and furniture Industry recorded as the highest growth rate of 14.2 per cent of capital during the entire study period. Paper, paper products and printing Industry found lowest growth rate as 11.8 per cent in the same period.

A pre and post transition period comparison depicts that there has been a decrease in the rate of growth of fixed capital for the entire Low Technology Manufacturing Sector from 17.5 per cent to 10.3 per cent during the post transition period. It is surprising to observe that despite of the adoption of liberalisation policies in the country, there has been a tremendous fall in the rate of growth of investment in fixed capital for all the industries. And also at disaggregate industries level all most all industries have been decreased in the post transition period. However, the highest growth rate of capital recorded in the Food, beverages and Tobacco Industry was 18.5 per cent and followed by Textiles, apparel and Leather Industry in the pre transition period. The lowest growth rate of capital found in the Paper, paper products and printing Industry to extent of 15.6.per cent in the same period

In all the industries growth rate of labour is lower than the value added and capital during the entire study period at the aggregate level. In most of the industries, the growth rate found negative during this period. A pre and post transition period comparison analysis suggests that trend growth rate of labour during Post transition period have decreased from 1.4 per cent to 0.6 per cent for Low Technology Manufacturing Sector at aggregate level. Textiles, apparel and Leather Industry recorded the highest growth rate of 1.0 per cent in of labour during the entire study period and the lowest growth rate was recorded in the Paper, paper products and printing Industry as -0.2 per cent in the Post transition period.

Growth Rates of Gross Value Added, Capital and Labour in Medium Low Technology Manufacturing Sector

The trend in the growth rates of GVA provided in the Table 3.11 stood at 4.6 per cent for aggregate Medium Low Technology Manufacturing Sector of the entire study period. In terms of Gross Value Added, Other manufacturing Industry was the best performer with highest growth rate of 15.6 per cent and followed by Petroleum refineries and Coal products Industry with 12.7 per cent rate of growth in the same period. On the contrary, the worst performing industry with lowest growth rate of -0.6 per cent in the Shipbuilding and repairing. A comparative analysis of pre and post transition periods declares that the growth rate was decreased and it was 7.3 per cent at pre transition period and fallen to 3.5 per cent in the post transition.

Out of 8 industrial groups, 3 industries have witnessed acceleration in the growth rate of GVA during the post transition period and the other five was not so. The highest growth rate of GVA was found in Petroleum refineries and Coal products the Industry to the extent of 14.1 in the post transition period and followed by Other Manufacturing Industry and Rubber and plastic products. And, the lowest growth rate of GVA was recorded with -12.1 per cent in the Shipbuilding and repairing in pre Transition period.

It has been noticed that growth rate of capital recorded as 13.3 per cent for aggregate level of Medium Low Technology Manufacturing Sector of the entire study period. The highest growth rate was recorded as 7. 1 per cent in the Other Manufacturing Industry during the entire study period and Shipbuilding and repairing industry had the lowest growth rate of capital with 3.9 per cent during the same period.

A pre and post transition period comparison depicts that the trend in growth rate of capital during post transition period have decreased from 17.6 per cent to 10.5 per cent for the entire Medium High Technology Manufacturing Sector. Almost all industries are witnessed acceleration in the growth rate of capital recorded in the pre Transition period.

The highest growth rate of capital was recorded 25.1 per cent in the Rubber and plastic products Industry and followed by Non- metallic mineral with growth rate of 22.4, and also Metal products industries with a growth rate of 20.2 in the pre transition period. The growth rate was found lowest growth rate of capital by Shipbuilding and repairing Industry to the extent of 1.1 per cent in pre transition period when compare to Post transition period.

Growth rate of labour is lower than the Gross Value Added and Capital in all the industries during the entire study period at the aggregate

Table 3.11: Compound Annual Growth Rates (CAGR) of Medium Low Technology Manufacturing Sector Pre & Post Transition period

Industry Group	*Value Added*			*Capital*			*Labour*		
	pre Transition period	*post Transition period*	*Entire period*	*pre Transition period*	*post Transition period*	*Entire period*	*pre Transition period*	*post Transition period*	*Entire period*
Rubber and plastic products	15.0	10.4	11.6	25.1	12.2	17.0	4.3	5.3	4.8
Shipbuilding and repairing	-12.1	8.3	-0.6	1.1	6.0	3.9	-10.1	1.5	-2.8
Other manufacturing	17.7	13.4	15.6	16.3	18.4	17.1	4.2	8.4	6.6
Non-ferrous metals	18.4	3.2	10.3	19.2	10.1	14.8	12.5	-7.5	1.2
Non-metallic mineral products	12.1	3.5	7.6	22.4	10.1	15.2	1.8	-0.2	0.9
Metal products	3.3	7.2	5.7	20.2	10.6	14.3	1.8	1.0	1.2
Petroleum refineries and coal products	13.1	14.1	12.7	16.8	17.1	16.7	2.4	2.9	2.5
Ferrous metals (Iron& steel)	4.7	10.2	5.3	15.5	7.8	11.0	-1.6	-1.1	-1.8
Aggregate	7.3	3.5	4.6	17.6	10.5	13.3	-0.9	0.9	-0.1

Source: Computed using the data from Annual Survey of Industries, EPW Research Foundation.

level. In most of the industries, the growth rate found less than two per cent during this period. A pre and post transition period comparison analysis suggests that the trend in growth rate of labour during post transition period has shows a positive result and it raised from -0.9 per cent to 0.9 per cent for Medium Low Technology Manufacturing Sector at aggregate level. Out of 8 industrial groups, 4 industries have witnessed acceleration in the growth rate of labour during the post transition period. The highest growth rate was found in the other Manufacturing Industries with 8.4 per cent. Whereas Non-ferrous metals Industry recorded as -7.5 per cent of negative growth rate of labour during the post transition period.

Chapter - IV

Economic Openness Impact on Indian Industrial Productivity [Pre and Post-Transition]

The Economic Openness has been undertaken since July, 1991 with the objective of increasing productivity and competitiveness of the domestic manufacturing sector. The process heralded the liberalisation of domestic industrial sector from various controls and regulations. There was a movement towards the establishment of a competitive market system with optimum resource utilisation. Under this process, the firms were exposed to international competition, which forced them introduce new methods of production, import quality inputs along with modern technology to improve their efficiency. The productivity of manufacturing sector has been a crucial factor to compete in the globalized world.

The significance of productivity, in increasing national welfare is now universally recognized. In every country, industry or organization, the main source of economic growth is a result of an increase in productivity. Nowadays, it is widely accepted that productivity is a key performance benchmark for any firm, involved in the manufacturing sector. This improvement in productivity is related to increased profitability, lower costs and sustainable competitiveness. Productivity[1] is defined as the efficient use of resources in the production of various goods and services. Rising productivity implies that either higher output is produced with the same amount of input or less input is required to produce the same level of output.

An attempt is being made to analyze the impact of Economic Openness on the productivity front. The domestic manufacturing sector based on technology classification is under purview. Technology classification - High Technology, Medium High Technology, Low Technology and Medium Low Technology Manufacturing Sectors [pre and post-transition 1981 to 1991 and 1991-2012] using the Malmquist Productivity Index.

The whole chapter has been divided into two broad sections. Section-I presents methodology containing non-parametric DEA Malmquist Productivity Index (MPI) approach to compute Total Factor Productivity (TFP) growth rates. Section-II deals with the empirical results related to the Inter-Industries Variations in TFP growth rate of domestic manufacturing sector. The Total Factor Productivity Change Index results are being calculated by using Data Envelopment Analysis Programme 2.1 (DEAP) linear programme developed by Coelli et.al (1998)[2].

Methodology Framework

The Data Envelopment Analysis (DEA) Model

In this study, Malmquist Productivity Index methods used to calculate Total Factor Productivity (TFP) of the Indian Manufacturing Sector based on technological classification. DEA based Malmquist productivity approach has been used extensively to measure performance in various sectors.

Data Envelopment Analysis (DEA) Advantages:

"The advantages of DEA briefly summarized by Majumdar (1997)[3] as follows:

- DEA is a multivariate technique that can take up multiple inputs and outputs into account. It can estimate Technical Efficiency and it is a non-parametric approach that does not require an assumption about the mathematical form of the production function.
- It is not necessary to make assumptions about the technology employed by firms.

- DEA carries out individual observation optimization because it is frontier oriented and does not estimate innermost tendencies. However, regression approaches use averaging technique and estimate a single parameter for all observations.
- DEA allows data set to be static or dynamic. The panel data estimates the optimum frontier for a firm with respect to efficiency characteristics of all Decision Making Units (DMUs) for that year.
- DEA can estimate scale efficiency without using the input prices."

Malmquist Total Factor Productivity (TFP) Index

Fare et al. (1982) defined the Malmquist Production Index by distance functions that are calculated by using Data Envelopment Analysis (DEA). DEA is a special mathematical linear programming model and test to assess efficiency and productivity. It allows use of panel data to estimate changes in total factor productivity and breaking it down into two components namely, Technological Change and Technical Efficiency Change. TFP growth measures how much productivity grows or declines over period of time. TFP grew when there were more outputs relative to the quantity of given inputs. It was so, when innovations such as electronics, improved design are called "Technological Change" were adapted[4]. TFP can grew, when the industry uses more efficiently the existing technology and economic inputs. They can produce more while using the same capital, labour and technology or by increasing "Technical Efficiency Change"[5]. TFP change from one year to the next is therefore comprised of Technological Change and Technical Efficiency Change.

This study uses the output-oriented model of DEA-Malmquist to put much weight on the expansion of output quantity out of a given amount of inputs. Therefore, TFP Index is a ratio of the weighted aggregate outputs to weighted aggregate inputs, using multiple outputs and inputs. The input and output quantities of industries were sets of data used to construct a piece-wise frontier over the data points. The efficiency measures were calculated related to this frontier that represents an efficient technology. The best-practice industry determines the production frontier, that is, those with highest level of production given a level of economic inputs. Points that lie below the piece-wise frontier were considered inefficient while points that lie on or above the frontier were efficient. The Malmquist approach was developed to combine inputs and outputs and then measure changes, following the use of many inputs with production of shared outputs. The Malmquist Index measures the Total Factor Productivity change between two data points over time, by calculating the ratio of distances of each data points relative to a common technology.

"DEA Malmquist TFP index is being used to calculate the ratio of the distances of each observation relative to the technology frontier and measure the TFP difference between two observations. The TFP change index for the ith DMU between the period t and period t+1 is defined by the Fare et al. (1994) as follows:

$$m_i(y_S, x_S, y_t, x_t,) = \left[\frac{d_i^t\left(y_i^{t+1}, x_i^{t+1}\right)}{d_i^{t+1}\left(y_i^t, x_i^{t+1}\right)} \times \frac{d_i^t\left(y_i^t, x_i^{t+1}\right)}{d_i^{t+1},\left(y_i^t, x_i^t\right)} \right]^{1/2}$$

y_i^t, x_i^{t+1} notion in the equation (1) represents the output produced by i[th] DMU during the period t and the input used by ith DMU during the period t+1, respectively. The $d_i^t\left(y_i^{t+1}, x_i^{t+1}\right)$ term in equation (1) refers to the distance between the observation at the period t+1 to the technology at the period t and $d_i^{t+1},\left(y_i^t, x_i^t\right)$ term represents the distance between the observation at the period t to the technology at the period t+1. If m_i is greater than one it indicates an increase in the TFP change from period t to period t+1. A value of m_i less than one point to a decrease in the TFP change from period t to period t+1 Equation (1) can be expressed as equation (2).

$$m_i\left(y_s, x_s, y_t, x_t\right) = \underbrace{\frac{d_i^t\left(y_i^{t+1}, x_i^{t+1}\right)}{d_i^t\left(y_i^t, x_i^t\right)}}_{\substack{\text{TECHNICAL EFFICIENCY}\\ \text{CHANGE (CHATCHING UP}\\ \text{EFFECT)}}} \times \underbrace{\left[\frac{d_i^t\left(y_i^{t+1}, x_i^{t+1}\right)}{d_i^{t+1}\left(y_i^{t+1}, x_i^{t+1}\right)} \times \frac{d_i^t\left(y_i^t, x_i^t\right)}{d_i^{t+1}\left(y_i^t, x_i^t\right)}\right]^{1/2}}_{\substack{\text{TECHNOLOGICAL}\\ \text{CHANGE (INNOVATION}\\ \text{EFFECT)}}}$$

In equation (2), the first multiplier is technical efficiency change between period's t and t+1 in the output-oriented model described by Farrell (1957)"[6]. It represents the ratio of the Technical Efficiency in period t to the technical efficiency in period t+1. The second multiplier in equation (2) corresponds to the technical change which is a geometric mean of the shift in the technology frontier between the period's t and t+1.

Empirical Findings

TFP Trends - High Technology Manufacturing Sector

The level of productivity growth is considered to be one of the most vital determinants of growth. The measurement and understanding of *Inter-Temporal and Inter-Industry* comparison of TFP growth can guide the policy makers for the formulation of a suitable policy for the rational resoûrce allocation and balanced regional development.

Table 4.1 and Table 4.2 provide *Inter-Temporal and Inter-Industry* comparison of Malmquist Productivity Index for the High Technology Manufacturing Sector. *Inter-Temporal* analysis reveals a cyclical fluctuation in the productivity growth of the High Technology Manufacturing Sector. The highest TFP growth rate recorded was 23.4 per cent [1994- 95] and the lowest TFP at -31.4 per cent [1998-99],

Table 4.2 reveals the productivity as positive in the sector at 0.398 per cent. It was maxima at 1.768 per cent [Office and Computing Equipment] and minima at -1.420 per cent [Drugs and Medicines]. The gestation period reflected the TFP growth for the sector at variance.

At the disaggregate level, TFP got improved from -4.275 per cent [pre transition] to 2.057 per cent [post-transition]. The Economic Openness, as such, seemed to impart somewhat positive with significant improvement. Almost all (two out of three) industries group, two industries showed some improvement [post-transition], except the drugs and medicines industry, where it swooped down. The industrial groups of office and computing equipments besides radio, t v and communications have had positive TFP [post-transition].

Table 4.1: Malmquist Productivity Index of High Technology Manufacturing Sector: An Inter-Temporal Analysis

Year	*Average MPI*	*Growth Rate*
1982-83	0.988	-1.2
1983-84	0.93	-7.5
1984-85	0.877	-14
1985-86	0.934	-7.1
1986-87	0.973	-2.8
1987-88	0.92	-8.7
1988-89	1.045	4.3
1989-90	1.117	10.5
1990-91	0.87	-14.9
1991-92	0.92	-8.7
1992-93	1.038	3.7
1993-94	0.991	-0.9
1994-95	1.305	23.4
1995-96	0.801	-24.8
1996-97	0.989	-1.1
1997-98	1.2	16.7
1998-99	0.761	-31.4
1999-00	1.033	3.2
2000-01	1.227	18.5
2001-02	0.915	-9.3
2002-03	1.176	15
2003-04	0.971	-3
2004-05	0.834	-19.9
2005-06	1.247	19.8
2006-07	0.816	-22.5
2007-08	0.902	-10.9
2008-09	1.317	24.1
2009-10	0.765	-30.7
2010-11	1.063	5.9
2011-12	0.909	-10

Source: Calculations by Data Envelopment Analysis Programme (DEAP), version 2.1.

Table 4.2: Malmquist Productivity Index of High Technology Manufacturing Sector: An Inter - Industry Change

Industry Group	Malmquist Productivity Index			Growth Rates		
	Pre Transition Period	Post Transition Period	Entire Period	Pre Transition Period	Post Transition Period	Entire Period
Office & Computing Equipment	0.905	1.081	1.018	-10.497	7.493	1.768
Drug &Medicines	1.013	0.956	0.986	1.283	-4.603	-1.420
Radio, TV &Communication	0.961	1.030	1.010	-4.058	2.913	0.990
Mean	0.959	1.021	1.004	-4.275	2.057	0.398

Source: Calculations by Data Envelopment Analysis Programme (DEAP), version 2.1.

Decomposition of TFP - High Technology Manufacturing Sector

The literature on MPI confirms that TFP growth can be bifurcated into two mutually exclusive and non- additive sources namely, Technical Efficiency Change and Technological Change. The Technical Efficiency Change component is a proxy of catching up whereas Technological Change represents a frontier shift.

Tables 4.3 and 4.4 provide the inter-temporal estimates of Technical Efficiency Change and Technological Change, respectively.

Table 4.3 explains that Technical Efficiency Change index is less than unitary mark for appreciable number of years under study. The behaviour of the coefficients of growth rate summarizes a mix of positive and negative pattern. Highest growth was at 16.6 per cent [1995-96]. Lowest growth was at -30.5 per cent [2011-12].

Table 4.4 explains the growth rate of technological change. It was maxima [1997-98] at 24.0 per cent [post-transition] and minima [1984-85] at -33.9 per cent [pre-transition].

Table 4.5 provides an *Inter-Industry* analysis of Technical Efficiency Change for the High Technology Manufacturing Sector. A comparative analysis of pre and post-transition suggests that office and computing equipment besides radio, t.v. and communication industries to have experienced improvements in the technical efficiency (from -7.181 per cent to 3.382 per cent and -2.145 per cent to 0.596 per cent) from pre-transition to post- transition, respectively. The drugs and medicines have experienced a striking decline in technical efficiency change, during the period.

Furthermore, Table 4.6 summarizes that out of three industries, only two categories i.e. office and computing as well as t.v. and communication have experienced the Technological Change post-transition while the drugs and medicines have not shifted their frontier.. the impact of Economic Openness on manufacturing sector has highlighted that strong positive technical change was observed for office and computing equipment industries.

TFP Sources - High Technology Manufacturing Sector

TFP growth sources ought to be known for better policy framework. The analysis for High Technology Manufacturing Sector exposes that (Tables: 4.2, 4.5, and 4.6) Technological Change and Technical Efficiency Change were at an average. At aggregate levels, the Technologic Change was beyond that of Technical Efficiency Change. It reflected the impact of Economic Openness (technology import after introduced economic reforms) to have been positive on the sector.

It increased from -4.2 per cent [pre transition] to 2.0 per cent [post-transition]. Technical Efficiency Change owed to such change.. Office and computing equipments as well as radio, t.v. and communication industries owe to the Technological Change dominates than Technical Efficiency Change. Technological Change as such was the major driving force of productivity improvement for those industries. However, the drugs and medicines witnessed Technical Efficiency Change beyond that of Technological Change.

TFP Trends - Medium High-technology Manufacturing Sector

An Inter-Temporal and Inter-Industry change was found witnessed by the sector w.r.t MPI and its components. The cyclical fluctuations were registered in the productivity growth behaviour during the study period. The growth was maxima at 14.3 per cent [1995-96], [Table 4.7] and minima at -52.9 per cent [2007-08]. Moreover, the index of productivity was less than unitary mark for a maximum number of times.

Further, in the case of Inter-Industry analysis, Table 4.8 replicates productivity as positive at 0.398 per cent for the sector. A further comparison of pre-transition to that of post- transition suggests an improvement in TFP growth. It was -1.937 per cent [pre-transition] and 2.629 per cent [post-transition]. TFP growth rate [post-transition] suggests the sector to have been responding positively against the Economic Openness based programmes initiated by the policy framers.

An Inter-Industrial analysis [Table 4.8] for the entire period of the sector showed chemicals and drugs to have maxima at 5.033 percent, followed by professional goods at 1.381 per cent and other transport at 1.283 per cent, whereas the non-electrical goods showed the poorest at -3.627.

The industries have responded quite well to the Economic Openness drive. The maxima was observed at 1.060 per cent for transport industry and the non-electrical industries was the worst sufferer.

Table 4.3: Technical Efficiency Index of High Technology Manufacturing Sector: An Inter-Temporal Analysis

Year	*Efficiency Change*	*Growth Rate*
1982-83	0.943	-6
1983-84	0.823	-21.5
1984-85	1.173	14.7
1985-86	0.937	-6.7
1986-87	1.043	4.1
1987-88	0.901	-11
1988-89	1.052	4.9
1989-90	1.042	4
1990-91	0.869	-15.1
1992-93	1.029	2.8
1993-94	0.862	-16

(Cont'd...)

1994-95	1.104	9.4
1995-96	1.199	16.6
1996-97	0.869	-15.1
1997-98	1.008	0.8
1998-99	0.811	-23.3
1999-00	1.068	6.4
2000-01	1.197	16.5
2001-02	0.944	-5.9
2002-03	1.045	4.3
2003-04	1.105	9.5
2004-05	0.77	-29.9
2005-06	1.022	2.2
2006-07	0.965	-3.6
2007-08	0.957	-4.5
2008-09	1.002	0.2
2009-10	0.886	-12.9
2010-11	1.179	15.2
2011-12	0.766	-30.5

Source: Calculations by Data Envelopment Analysis Programme (DEAP), version 2.1.

Table 4.4: Technological Change Index of High Technology Manufacturing Sector: An Inter-Temporal Analysis

Year	*Technological Change*	*Growth Rate*
1982-83	1.048	4.6
1983-84	1.13	11.5
1984-85	0.747	-33.9
1985-86	0.997	-0.3
1986-87	0.933	-7.2
1987-88	1.021	2.1

(Cont'd...)

1988-89	0.994	-0.6
1989-90	1.072	6.7
1990-91	1.001	0.1
1991-92	0.967	-3.4
1992-93	1.009	0.9
1993-94	1.15	13
1994-95	1.182	15.4
1995-96	0.668	-49.7
1996-97	1.138	12.1
1997-98	1.191	16
1998-99	0.938	-6.6
1999-00	0.967	-3.4
2000-01	1.025	2.4
2001-02	0.97	-3.1
22002-03	1.125	11.1
2003-04	0.879	-13.8
2004-05	1.083	7.7
2005-06	1.219	18
2006-07	0.846	-18.2
2007-08	0.942	-6.2
2008-09	1.315	24
2009-10	0.863	-15.9
2010-11	0.902	-10.9
2011-12	1.186	15.7

Source: Calculations by Data Envelopment Analysis Programme (DEAP), version 2.1.

Table 4.5: Technical Efficiency Change Index of High Technology Manufacturing Sector: An Inter- Industry Analysis

Industry Group	*Technical Efficiency Index*			*Growth Rates*		
	Pre Transition Period	*Post Transition Period*	*Entire Period*	*Pre Transition Period*	*Post Transition Period*	*Entire Period*
Office & Computing Equipment	0.933	1.035	1.000	-7.181	3.382	0.000
Drug & Medicines	1.000	0.997	0.998	0.000	-0.301	-0.200
Radio, TV & Communication	0.979	1.006	1.000	-2.145	0.596	0.000
Mean	0.970	1.013	1.000	-3.093	1.283	0.000

Source: Calculations by Data Envelopment Analysis Programme (DEAP), version 2.1.

Table 4.6: Technological Change Index of High Technology Manufacturing Sector: An Inter- Industry Analysis

Industry Group	*Technological Change Index*			*Growth Rates*		
	Pre Transition Period	*Post Transition Period*	*Entire Period*	*Pre Transition Period*	*Post Transition Period*	*Entire Period*
Office & Computing Equipment	0.970	1.045	1.017	-3.093	4.306	1.672
Drug &Medicines	1.013	0.959	0.987	1.283	-4.275	-1.317
Radio, TV &Communication	0.981	1.023	1.010	-1.937	2.248	0.990
Mean	0.988	1.008	1.005	-1.215	0.794	0.498

Source: Calculations by Data Envelopment Analysis Programme (DEAP), version 2.1.

Table 4.7: Malmquist Productivity Index of Medium High Technology Manufacturing Sector: An Inter-Temporal Analysis

Year	*Average MPI*	*Growth Rate*
1982-83	1.002	0.2
1983-84	0.972	-2.9
1984-85	0.935	-7
1985-86	0.892	-12.1
1986-87	0.97	-3.1
1987-88	1.003	0.3
1988-89	0.977	-2.4
1989-90	1.007	0.7
1990-91	1.087	8
1991-92	1.112	10.1
1992-93	0.972	-2.9
1993-94	1.056	5.3
1994-95	1.108	9.7
1995-96	1.167	14.3
1996-97	0.908	-10.1
1997-98	0.889	-12.5
1998-99	1.127	11.3
1999-00	1.023	2.2
2000-01	0.866	-15.5
2001-02	1.112	10.1
2002-03	1.007	0.7
2003-04	1.155	13.4
2004-05	1.067	6.3
2005-06	0.98	-2.0
2006-07	0.985	-1.5
2007-08	0.654	-52.9
2008-09	1.076	7.1
2009-10	1.045	4.3
2010-11	1.102	9.3
2011-12	0.988	-1.2

Source: Calculations by Data Envelopment Analysis Programme (DEAP), version 2.1.

Table 4.8: Malmquist Productivity Index of Medium-High Technology Manufacturing Sector: An Inter- Industry Analysis

Industry Group	*Malmquist Productivity Index*			*Growth Rate*		
	Pre Transition Period	*Post Transition Period*	*Entire Period*	*Pre Transition Period*	*Post Transition Period*	*Entire Period*
Professional goods	0.952	1.055	1.014	-5.042	5.213	1.381
Motor vehicles	0.990	1.012	0.996	-1.010	1.186	-0.402
Electrical machines excl.com equipment	0.982	1.000	0.986	-1.833	0.000	-1.420
Chemicals excl. drugs	1.084	1.041	1.053	7.749	3.939	5.033
Other transport	0.960	1.060	1.013	-4.167	5.660	1.283
Non-electrical	0.927	1.000	0.965	-7.875	0.000	-3.627
Mean	0.981	1.027	1.004	-1.937	2.629	0.398

Source: Calculations by Data Envelopment Analysis Programme (DEAP), version 2.1.

Decomposition of TFP - Medium High Technology Manufacturing Sector

As mentioned earlier, MPI growth could be attributed to two mutually exclusive and non additive sources, namely, Catching up Effect and Shift in Frontier. Table 4.9 provides the inter-temporal estimates of Technical Efficiency Change in the Medium High Technology Manufacturing Sector.

Table 4.9 portrays the Technical Efficiency Change as less than unitary mark for appreciable number of years under study. The growth ranged between 17.4 per cent maxima (1985-86) and -38.7 per cent minima (2008-09). The Inter-Industry analysis of the Table 4.10 showed the positive Technical Efficiency Change for professional goods, motor vehicles, and other transport vehicles, while motor vehicles, electrical machines excluding communication equipments and non-electrical industries were under regress.

Technical Efficiency Change was found improved pre and post-transition for the sector. It was -1.317 per cent [pre-transition] and 0.695 per cent [post-transition] Inter-Industrial analysis, as such, revealed the professional goods showed maxima at 3.475 followed by other transport vehicles [3.195 per cent] while electrical machines excluding communication equipment [-2.249 per cent].

Inter-Temporal and Inter-Industry results for Technological Change were reported in the Tables 4.11 and 4.12. Table 4.11 delineates the cyclical trends for Technological Change in the sector for the study period. The highest growth rate (17.3 per cent) in terms of Technological Change was witnessed [2001-02], while the lowest growth rate (-43.5 per cent) was observed [2004-05].

The Inter-Industry Table 4.12 pertains to Technological Change. The professional goods, electrical machines excluding communication equipment and non-electrical goods showed negative growth while other industries of the sector showed positive growth for the study period. Chemicals and drugs industry was the highest at 4.762 per cent in the Technological Change whereas the technical regress was at -1.908 per cent for non-electrical industry followed by similar growth for professional goods industry in the sector.

A comparative analysis of Inter-Industry change for pre and post-transition showed an improvement in Technological Change in all the industries except motor vehicles and chemicals and drugs, where the growth fell from 2.818 per cent to 0.299 per cent and 7.149 per cent to 3.939 per cent [post-transition] respectively.

Technological Change for the study period with the sector stood at 0.299 per cent [post-transition]. It was higher and positive during the Economic Openness than the Closed Economy. Introduction of new and advanced technology has certainly benefitted the sector exposed to Economic Openness.

TFP Sources - Medium High Technology Manufacturing Sector

At aggregate level, (Table: 4.8, 4.10 and 4.12), the Technological Change is greater than Technical Efficiency Change, justifying the TFP growth on the shift in the frontier rather than the improvement in efficiency. The Economic Openness had had positive impact on the sector.

TFP growth was 1.9 per cent [pre-transition] and 2.7 per cent [post-transition] in the sector due to Technological Change. Economic Openness, as such, had positive impact on the sector productivity.

At Disaggregate level, the inter-industry analysis for all industries remained positive. The source of TFP growth was an average for Technological Change and Technical Efficiency Change. Professional goods, motor vehicles and other transport industries owed to Technical Efficiency Change, with an index, the growth ranged from 1.009 to 1.036. This result depicts the growth to have been boosted by the enhancement of productivity based on catching-up capability, specifically on the effective use of human capital. For other industries like chemicals excluding drugs, non-electrical, electrical machines excluding communication equipment industries the source of TFP growth was Technology Change, with index scores of 1.041, 1.033 and 1.023, respectively. The result reflects that level of technology in these industries was still moderate and technological adoption could take place much easier.

Table 4.9: Efficiency Changes of Index - Medium High Technology Manufacturing Sector: An Inter Temporal Analysis

Year	*Efficiency Change*	*Growth Rate*
1982-83	0.996	-0.4
1983-84	0.993	-0.7
1984-85	0.836	-19.6
1985-86	1.211	17.4
1986-87	0.983	-1.7
1987-88	0.904	-10.6
1988-89	1.037	3.6
1989-90	0.925	-8.1
1990-91	1.035	3.4
1991-92	1.109	9.8
1992-93	0.933	-7.2
1993-94	1.138	12.1
1994-95	0.987	-1.3
1995-96	1.079	7.3
1996-97	1.064	6

(Cont'd...)

1997-98	0.819	-22.1
1998-99	1.069	6.5
1999-00	1.109	9.8\
2000-01	1.019	1.9
2001-02	0.92	-8.7
2002-03	0.966	-3.5
2003-04	1.024	2.3
2004-05	0.975	-2.6
2005-06	1.14	12.3
2006-07	0.943	-6.0
2007-08	1.012	1.2
2008-09	0.721	-38.7
2009-10	1.077	7.1
2010-11	1.132	11.7
2011-12	1.007	0.7

Source: Calculations by Data Envelopment Analysis Programme (DEAP), version 2.1.

Table 4.10: Technical Efficiency Index - Medium- High Technology Manufacturing Sector: An Inter- Industry Analysis

Industry Group	*Efficiency Change*			*Growth rates*		
	Pre Transition Period	*Post Transition Period*	*Entire Period*	*Pre Transition Period*	*Post Transition Period*	*Entire Period*
Professional goods	1.007	1.036	1.034	0.695	3.475	3.288
Motor vehicles	0.963	1.009	0.990	-3.842	0.892	-1.010
Electrical machines excl.com equipment	1.000	0.978	0.988	0.000	-2.249	-1.215
Chemicals excl. Drugs	1.007	1.000	1.003	0.695	0.000	0.299
Other transport	0.970	1.033	1.009	-3.093	3.195	0.892
Non-electrical	0.974	0.986	0.984	-2.669	-1.420	-1.626
Mean	0.987	1.007	1.001	-1.317	0.695	0.100

Source: Calculations by Data Envelopment Analysis Programme (DEAP), version 2.1.

Table 4.11: Technological Changes Index - Medium High Technology Manufacturing Sector: An Inter-Temporal Analysis

Year	*Technological Change*	*Growth Rate*
1982-83	1.006	0.6
1983-84	0.979	-2.1
1984-85	1.118	10.6
1985-86	0.737	-35.7
1986-87	0.987	-1.3
1987-88	1.11	9.9
1988-89	0.941	-6.3
1989-90	1.088	8.1
1990-91	1.05	4.8
1991-92	1.094	8.6
1992-93	1.043	4.1
1993-94	0.928	-7.8
1994-95	1.123	11
1995-96	1.082	7.6
1996-97	0.854	-17.1
1997-98	1.086	7.9
1998-99	1.054	5.1
1999-00	0.923	-8.3
2000-01	0.85	-17.6
2001-02	1.209	17.3
2002-03	1.043	4.1
2003-04	1.127	11.3
2004-05	0.697	-43.5
2005-06	0.935	-7.0
2006-07	1.039	3.8
2007-08	0.974	-2.7
2008-09	0.906	-10.4
2009-10	0.999	-0.1
2010-11	0.923	-8.3
2011-12	1.094	8.6

Source: Calculations by Data Envelopment Analysis Programme (DEAP), version 2.1.

Table 4.12: Technological Change Index - Medium- High Technology Manufacturing Sector: An Inter- Industry Analysis

Industry Group	*Technological Change Index*			*Growth Rate*		
	Pre Transition Period	*Post Transition Period*	*Entire Period*	*Pre Transition Period*	*Post Transition Period*	*Entire Period*
Professional goods	0.946	1.018	0.981	-5.708	1.768	-1.937
Motor vehicles	1.029	1.003	1.006	2.818	0.299	0.596
Electrical machines excl.com equipment	0.982	1.023	0.998	-1.833	2.248	-0.200
Chemicals excl. drugs	1.077	1.041	1.050	7.149	3.939	4.762
Other transport	0.990	1.026	1.004	-1.010	2.534	0.398
Non-electrical	0.952	1.014	0.981	-5.042	1.381	-1.937
Mean	0.995	1.021	1.003	-0.503	2.057	0.299

Source: Calculations by Data Envelopment Analysis Programme (DEAP), version 2.1.

TFP Trends - Low-Technology Manufacturing Sector

Table 4.13 and 4.14 provides inter-temporal and inter-industry comparison of Malmquist Productivity Index for the Sector. Inter-temporal analysis reflected cyclical fluctuations in the TFP growth for the sector. TFP growth was maxima at 23.5 per cent [2004-05] and minima at -25.5 per cent [1992-93]. MPI was less than unitary mark, explaining the poor level of productivity. Table 4.14 reflected the TFP growth rate for the sector under regress at -1.626 per cent during the study period. Paper, paper products and the printing industry had the highest TFP at 1.186 per cent, while wood products, furniture, textiles, apparel and leather besides food, beverages and tobacco industries stood negative TFP over the study period.

Table 4.13: Malmquist Productivity Index - Low Technology Industry: An Inter-Temporal Analysis

Year	*Average MPI*	*Growth Rate*
1982-83	0.908	-10.1
1983-84	1.082	7.6
1984-85	1.033	3.2
1985-86	0.922	-8.5
1986-87	1.025	2.4
1987-88	0.953	-4.9
1988-89	1.071	6.6
1989-90	1.06	5.7
1990-91	1.069	6.5
1991-92	1.048	4.6
1992-93	0.797	-25.5
1993-94	1.088	8.1
1994-95	0.953	-4.9
1995-96	0.897	-11.5
1996-97	1.076	7.1
1997-98	0.83	-20.5
1998-99	1.043	4.1
1999-00	1.121	10.8
2000-01	0.968	-3.3
2001-02	0.96	-4.2
2002-03	0.978	-2.2
2003-04	0.97	-3.1
2004-05	1.308	23.5
2005-06	1.186	15.7
2006-07	0.938	-6.6
2007-08	0.989	-1.1
2008-09	1.048	4.6
2009-10	1.117	10.5
2010-11	1.209	17.3
2011-12	1.237	19.2

Source: Calculations by Data Envelopment Analysis Programme (DEAP), version 2.1.

Table 4.14: Malmquist Productivity Index - Low Technology Manufacturing Sector: An Inter- Industry Analysis

Industry Group	*Malmquist Productivity Index*			*Growth Rate*		
	Pre Transition Period	*Post Transition Period*	*Entire Period*	*Pre Transition Period*	*Post Transition Period*	*Entire Period*
Paper, paper products and printing	1.015	1.017	1.012	1.478	1.672	1.186
Textiles, apparel and leather	1.019	0.984	0.994	1.865	-1.626	-0.604
Food, beverages and tobacco	1.046	0.968	0.999	4.398	-3.306	-0.100
Wood products and furniture	0.968	0.909	0.935	-3.306	-10.011	-6.952
Mean	1.012	0.969	0.984	1.186	-3.199	-1.626

Source: Calculations by Data Envelopment Analysis Programme (DEAP), version 2.1.

A comparison of pre and post-transition for the sector on the impact of Economic Openness showed TFP growth was under regress. It was at 1.186 per cent [pre-transition] and -3.199 [post-transition] An Inter-Industrial analysis reveals that the paper, paper products, and painting industry have reported the TFP at 1.672 while wood products and the furniture industry have suffered the worst with TFP growth at -10.011 [post-transition]. The performance for textiles, apparels and leather, food, beverages and tobacco, as well as wood products and furniture [post-transition] were under regress out of four industries.

Decomposition of TFP: Low Technology Manufacturing Sector

Table 4.15 portrays the inter-temporal estimates of Technical Efficiency Change hung at less than unitary mark for the study period. TFP was maxima at 30 per cent [2006-07] and was minima at – 56 per cent [2004-05]. The Inter-Industry analysis provided in the Table 4.16 depicts that food, beverages, and tobacco industry, the Technical Efficiency change was positive. Other industries have seldom witnessed any change which applied for paper, paper products, painting, textiles, apparels and leather, as well as wood products and furniture.

At aggregate level, textiles, apparel, and leather industry has experienced improvement in Technical Efficiency Change [pre- to post-transition], respectively. Other industries remained constant without any change.

Analyses of Inter-Temporal and Inter-Industry result for Technological Change are reported in the Tables 4.17 and 4.18. Table 4.17 describes the cyclical trend for Technological Change in the sector for the study period. The growth was maxima at 29.4 per cent [2010-11]; minima at -52.7 per cent [2006-07]. The inter-industry analysis of the study period has paper, paper products and the painting industry for positive level of Technological Change, while textiles, apparel and leather, food, beverage, and tobacco, as well as wood products and furniture for negative level.

A comparative analysis of Inter-Industry change pre- and post-transition periods reveals that there has been regress in Technological Change in all the industries except. paper, paper products and painting. TFP growth between the pre and post-transition has increased from 1.478 per cent to 1.672 per cent.

Table 4.15: Efficiency Changes - Low Technology Manufacturing Sector: An Inter-Temporal Analysis

Year	*Efficiency Change*	*Growth rate*
1982-83	1.115	10.3
1983-84	1.031	3
1984-85	0.977	-2.4
1985-86	1.099	9
1986-87	0.995	-0.5
1987-88	0.956	-4.6
1988-89	1.003	0.3
1989-90	1.045	4.3
1990-91	0.877	-14
1991-92	0.949	-5
1992-93	1.185	15.6
1993-94	0.976	-2.5

(Cont'd...)

1994-95	0.981	-1.9
1995-96	0.951	-5.2
1996-97	1.039	3.8
1997-98	0.952	-5
1998-99	0.936	-6.8
1999-00	1.16	13.8
2000-01	0.944	-5.9
2001-02	1.011	1.1
2002-03	1.01	1
2003-04	0.975	-2.6
2004-05	0.64	-56
2005-06	0.862	-16
2006-07	1.433	30
2007-08	1.132	12
2008-09	0.899	-11
2009-10	0.949	-5
2010-11	0.853	-17
2011-12	1.045	4.3

Source: Calculations by Data Envelopment Analysis Programme, version 2.1.

TFP Sources - Low Technology Manufacturing Sector

At the aggregate level, Table: 4.14, 4.16 and 4.18 shows the TFP growth of the sector was negative owing to negative contribution from Technological Change. However, Technical Efficiency Change was positive with an index growth of 1.007.

The analysis of the impact of Economic Openness on TFP growth in the sector reflected it to have fallen from 1.2 per cent [pre-transition] to -3.1 percent [post-transition]. The major source for productivity regress was Technological Change [post-transition]. Inter- industry analysis revealed the industries under evaluation, there was a regress in TFP growth rate. Technological Change was a major source of sluggishness in productivity [post-transition] in contrast with the growth [pre-transition]. Paper, paper products and printing industry had progressive growth [post-transition] in contrast with that [pre transition] due to Technological Change.

Table 4.16: Efficiency Change Index - Low Technology Manufacturing Sector: An Inter- Industry Analysis

Industry Group	*Efficiency Change*			*Growth Rate*		
	Pre Transition Period	*Post Transition Period*	*Entire Period*	*Pre Transition Period*	*Post Transition Period*	*Entire Period*
Paper, paper products and printing	1.000	1.000	1.000	0.000	0.000	0.000
Textiles, apparel and leather	1.000	1.008	1.001	0.000	0.794	0.100
Food, beverages and tobacco	1.034	1.021	1.026	3.288	2.057	2.534
Wood products and furniture	1.000	1.000	1.000	0.000	0.000	0.000
Mean	1.008	1.007	1.007	0.794	0.695	0.695

Source: Calculations by Data Envelopment Analysis Programme, version 2.1.

Table 4.17: Technological Changes Index - Low Technology Manufacturing Sector: An Inter-Temporal Analysis

Year	*Technological Change*	*Growth Rate*
1982-83	0.814	-22.9
1983-84	1.05	4.8
1984-85	1.058	5.5
1985-86	0.838	-19.3
1986-87	1.031	3
1987-88	0.997	-0.3
1988-89	1.068	6.4
1989-90	1.015	1.5
1990-91	1.219	18
1991-92	1.05	4.8
1992-93	0.673	-48.6
1993-94	1.115	10.3
1994-95	0.971	-3

(Cont'd...)

1995-96	0.943	-6
1996-97	1.035	3.4
1997-98	0.872	-14.7
1998-99	1.114	10.2
1999-00	0.966	-3.5
2000-01	1.025	2.4
2001-02	0.949	-5.4
2002-03	0.968	-3.3
2003-04	0.994	-0.6
2004-05	1.068	6.4
2005-06	1.376	27.3
2006-07	0.655	-52.7
2007-08	0.874	-14.4
2008-09	1.165	14.2
2009-10	1.177	15.0
2010-11	1.417	29.4
2011-12	1.015	1.5

Source: Calculations by Data Envelopment Analysis Programme, version 2.1.

Table 4.18: Technological Change Index - Low Technology Manufacturing Sector: An Inter- Industry Analysis

Industry Group	*Technological Change*			*Growth Rate*		
	Pre Transition Period	*Post Transition Period*	*Entire Period*	*Pre Transition Period*	*Post Transition Period*	*Entire Period*
Paper, paper products and printing	1.015	1.017	1.012	1.478	1.672	1.186
Textiles, apparel and leather	1.019	0.976	0.993	1.865	-2.459	-0.705
Food, beverages and tobacco	1.012	0.948	0.974	1.186	-5.485	-2.669
Wood products and furniture	0.968	0.909	0.935	-3.306	-10.011	-6.952
Mean	1.003	0.962	0.978	0.299	-3.950	-2.249

Source: Calculations by Data Envelopment Analysis Programme, version 2.1.

TFP Trends - Medium Low Technology Manufacturing Sector

Tables 4.19 and 4.20 provide Inter-Temporal and Inter-Industry comparison of Malmquist Productivity Index for the sector. The Inter-Temporal analysis reveals that cyclical fluctuation in the productivity growth. TFP growth rate was highest at 11.7 per cent [1999-00] whereas it was the lowest at -19.6 per cent [1986-87]. The Inter-Industries analysis of Table 4.20 depicts the TFP growth of the sector at 0.695 during the entire study period. Petroleum refineries and coal products industry had highest TFP growth at 5.749 per cent whereas metal products industry recorded lowest TFP growth with -2.041. The comparison of pre and post-transition periods revealed that TFP growth rate in the sector increased from -0.806 per cent (pre-transition period) to 2.344 percent (post-transition period).

Table 4.19: Malmquist Productivity Index - Medium Low Technology Manufacturing Sector: An Inter-Temporal Analysis

Year	*Average MPI*	*Growth Rate*
1982-83	1.027	2.6
1983-84	0.936	-6.8
1984-85	1.073	6.8
1985-86	1.115	10.3
1986-87	0.836	-19.6
1987-88	1.025	2.4
1988-89	1.008	0.8
1989-90	0.972	-2.9
1990-91	0.965	-3.6
1991-92	1.076	7.1
1992-93	1.052	4.9
1993-94	1.122	10.9
1994-95	0.97	-3.1
1995-96	1.061	5.7
1996-97	0.906	-10.4
1997-98	1.027	2.6
1998-99	1.049	4.7
1999-00	1.132	11.7

(Cont'd...)

2000-01	0.852	-17.4
2001-02	1.067	6.3
2002-03	1.076	7.1
2003-04	1.014	1.4
2004-05	0.893	-12.0
2005-06	1.016	1.6
2006-07	1.115	10.3
2007-08	1.08	7.4
2008-09	1.009	0.9
2009-10	0.838	-19.3
2010-11	0.977	-2.4
2011-12	0.935	-7.0

Source: Calculations by Data Envelopment Analysis Programme, version 2.1.

Table 4.20: Malmquist Productivity Index of Medium- Low Technology: An Inter- Industry Analysis

Industry Group	*Malmquist Productivity Index*			*Growth Rate*		
	Pre Transition Period	*Post Transition Period*	*Entire Period*	*Pre Transition Period*	*Post Transition Period*	*Entire Period*
Rubber and plastic products	1.006	1.004	1.001	0.596	0.398	0.100
Shipbuilding and repairing	0.926	1.056	0.998	-7.991	5.303	-0.200
Other manufacturing	1.002	0.998	1.018	0.200	-0.200	1.768
Non-ferrous metals	1.024	1.014	1.018	2.344	1.381	1.768
Non-metallic mineral products	1.010	0.982	0.998	0.990	-1.833	-0.200
Metal products	0.921	1.020	0.980	-8.578	1.961	-2.041
Petroleum refineries and coal products	1.109	1.064	1.061	9.829	6.015	5.749
Ferrous metals (Iron& steel)	0.950	1.059	0.987	-5.263	5.571	-1.317
Mean	0.992	1.024	1.007	-0.806	2.344	0.695

Source: Calculations by Data Envelopment Analysis Programme, version 2.1.

However, at disaggregated Inter- Industry analysis has been observed at the productivity, an improvement among different industries namely: Shipbuilding and repairing, Metal products, Petroleum refineries and coal products, and Ferrous metals (Iron& steel). Among eight industries, three industries are regress of their productivity performance such as Rubber and plastic products, Other manufacturing and Non-ferrous metals industries during post transition period in comparison to pre transition period.

Decomposition of TFP of Medium Low Technology Manufacturing Sector

Tables 4.21 and 4.22 provide the Inter-Temporal estimates of Technical Efficiency Change and Technological Change, respectively. Table 4.21 explains that Technical Efficiency Change Index is less than unitary mark for appreciable number of years in the entire study period. The behaviour of the coefficients of growth rates summarizes a mixed trend of positive and negative pattern. The growth rate ranges between a maximum of 39.2 per cent growth (2002-03) and a minimum of -83.8 per cent (1985-86) for the sector.

Table 4.21: Efficiency Changes index - Medium Low Technology Manufacturing Sector: An Inter-Temporal Analysis

Year	*Efficiency Change*	*Growth Rate*
1982-83	1.035	3.4
1983-84	1.092	8.4
1984-85	1.05	4.8
1985-86	0.544	-83.8
1986-87	1.325	24.5
1987-88	0.921	-8.6
1988-89	1.14	12.3
1989-90	0.91	-9.9
1990-91	1.172	14.7
1991-92	1.076	7.1
1992-93	0.843	-18.6

(Cont'd...)

1993-94	0.802	-24.7
1994-95	1.246	19.7
1995-96	1.004	0.4
1996-97	0.976	-2.5
1997-98	1.301	23.1
1998-99	0.992	-0.8
1999-00	0.914	-9.4
2000-01	1.115	10.3
2001-02	0.639	-56.5
2002-03	1.644	39.2
2003-04	0.95	-5.3
2004-05	0.954	-4.8
2005-06	0.759	-31.8
2006-07	1.025	2.4
2007-08	0.99	-1.0
2008-09	1.009	0.9
2009-10	1.057	5.4
2010-11	0.941	-6.3
2011-12	1.151	13.1

Source: Calculations by Data Envelopment Analysis Programme, version 2.1.

Table 4.22: Technological Changes index - Medium Low Technology Manufacturing Sector: An Inter-Temporal Analysis

Year	***Technological Change***	***Growth Rate***
1982-83	0.992	-0.8
1983-84	0.857	-16.7
1984-85	1.022	2.2
1985-86	2.051	51.2
1986-87	0.631	-58.5
1987-88	1.113	10.2
1988-89	0.884	-13.1

(Cont'd...)

1989-90	1.068	6.4
1990-91	0.823	-21.5
1991-92	1.172	14.7
1992-93	1.248	19.9
1993-94	1.4	28.6
1994-95	0.779	-28.4
1995-96	1.056	5.3
1996-97	0.928	-7.8
1997-98	0.789	-26.7
1998-99	1.057	5.4
1999-00	1.238	19.2
2000-01	0.764	-30.9
2001-02	1.67	40.1
2002-03	0.654	-52.9
2003-04	1.067	6.3
2004-05	0.935	-7.0
2005-06	1.339	25.3
2006-07	1.088	8.1
2007-08	1.091	8.3
2008-09	1.00	0.0
2009-10	0.793	-26.1
2010-11	1.039	3.8
2011-12	0.813	-23.0

Source: Calculations by Data Envelopment Analysis Programme, version 2.1.

On the other hand, Table 4.22 depicts an analysis of Inter-Temporal results for Technological Change. The optimum growth rate of Technological Change was found at 28.6 per cent [1993-94 post transition period, while the lowest growth rate was at -58.5 per cent [1986-87] during pre-transition period.

Table 4.23: Efficiency Change Index - Medium- Low Technology Manufacturing Sector: An Inter- Industry Analysis

Industry Group	*Efficiency Change*			*Growth Rate*		
	Pre Transition Period	*Post Transition Period*	*Entire Period*	*Pre Transition Period*	*Post Transition Period*	*Entire Period*
Rubber and plastic products	1.008	1.006	1.009	0.794	0.596	0.892
Shipbuilding and repairing	0.920	1.032	0.985	-8.696	3.101	-1.523
Other manufacturing	1.103	1.000	1.041	9.338	0.000	3.939
Non-ferrous metals	1.013	0.988	1.005	1.283	-1.215	0.498
Non-metallic mineral products	1.010	0.974	0.998	0.990	-2.669	-0.200
Metal products	0.990	1.005	0.993	-1.010	0.498	-0.705
Petroleum refineries and coal products	1.000	1.000	1.000	0.000	0.000	0.000
Ferrous metals (Iron& steel)	0.929	1.052	0.991	-7.643	4.943	-0.908
Mean	0.995	1.007	1.003	-0.503	0.695	0.299

Source: Calculations by Data Envelopment Analysis Programme, version 2.1.

Table 4.23 provides an inter-industry analysis of Technical Efficiency Change for the sector. At disaggregate level, except ship building and repairing, non-metallic mineral products, metal products and ferrous metals (iron and steel) other industries have an efficiency regress and while other industries were in progress for the study period.

A comparison analysis of pre and post-transition period reveals that at efficiency front, an improvement has been noticed from 0.503 per cent [pre transition] was up to 0.695 percent in the post-transition period. Furthermore, ferrous metals (iron and steel) and ship building and repairing had more improvement. The petroleum refineries and coal products industry has no Efficiency Change [pre and post-transition].

Table 4.24: Technological Change Index - Medium- Low Technology Manufacturing Sector: An Inter- Industry Analysis

Industry Group	*Technological Change*			*Growth Rate*		
	Pre Transition Period	*Post Transition Period*	*Entire Period*	*Pre Transition Period*	*Post Transition Period*	*Entire Period*
Rubber and plastic products	0.998	0.998	0.992	-0.200	-0.200	-0.806
Shipbuilding and repairing	1.006	1.023	1.013	0.596	2.248	1.283
Other manufacturing	0.909	0.998	0.978	-10.011	-0.200	-2.249
Non-ferrous metals	1.011	1.026	1.013	1.088	2.534	1.283
Non-metallic mineral products	1.001	1.009	1.000	0.100	0.892	0.000
Metal products	0.931	1.015	0.988	-7.411	1.478	-1.215
Petroleum refineries and coal products	1.109	1.064	1.061	9.829	6.015	5.749
Ferrous metals (Iron& steel)	1.023	1.007	0.996	2.248	0.695	-0.402
Mean	0.997	1.017	1.005	-0.301	1.672	0.498

Source: Calculations by Data Envelopment Analysis Programme, version 2.1.

Table 4.24 deals with an Inter-Industries analysis of Technological Change of the sector depicts that rubber and plastic products, other manufacturing, metal products and ferrous metals (iron and steel) are in regress and the rest of other industries reported positive TFP of for Technological Change for the study period. The petroleum refineries and coal products industry has observed the highest Technical Change at 5.749 per cent, whereas other manufacturing industry was found to be worst performer at -2.249 per cent. Table 4.24 summarizes the sector had rise in the rate of Technological Change from -0.301 per cent [pre transition] to 1.672 per cent [post-transition] reflected positive growth for industries (expect rubber and plastic products) under evaluation.

TFP Sources - Medium Low Technology Manufacturing Sector

The analysis of the sources of the TFP growth in Medium Low Technology Manufacturing Sector reveals that (refer Table: 4.20, 4.23

and 4.24) an average both Technological Change and Technical Efficiency Change are equally contributing TFP growth in this sector. It has been observed that at aggregate level, the Technological Change was greater than Efficiency Change, which implies the growth in TFP owes to shift in the frontier rather than improvement in efficiency. Hence, the study suggests that a positive impact of Economic Openness on technological advancement of the sector. The analysis of the impact of Economic Openness on TFP growth revealed the TFP growth in the sector to have increased -0.8 per cent [pre transition] to 2.4 per cent [post-transition]. Hence, at aggregated levels, the impact of Economic Openness was positive. The main source of TFP growth owes to Technological Change. The Inter-industry analysis revealed among all the industries, rubber and plastic products, other manufacturing industry, non-ferrous metals, non- metal products and petroleum refineries and coal products growth rate posted positive TFP [pre- transition compared to post-transition]. Technical Efficiency Change on an average had been the driver of TFP growth [pre-transition], whereas remaining industries were positive [post- transition]. TFP growth source owes to Technical Efficiency Change.

References

1. There are three principal approaches to measurement of productivity growth. Those are :(i) The index number approach, (ii) parametric approach and (iii) non-parametric approach, In this study productivity growth estimated using the non-parametric approach which is based on linear programming model.
2. Coelli T.J, A Guide to DEAP Version 2.1: "*A Data Envelopment Analysis (computer program) CEAP*" working paper 96/08, Department of Econometrics, University of New England, Australia.
3. Majumdar, S., (1997), "Incentive regulation and productive efficiency in the U.S telecommunication industry", *Journal of Business* 70, pp. 547-576.
4. Technological Change is the development of new products or the development of new technologies that allows methods of production to improve and results in the shifting upwards of the production frontier. More specifically, Technological Change includes a new production process which is called process of innovation and the discoveries of new products are called products of innovation.
5. On the other hand, can make use of existing labour, capital, and other economic inputs to produce more of same product. An example is increase

in skill or learning by doing. As producers gain experience at producing something they become more and more efficient at it. Labour find new ways of doing things so that relatively minor modifications to plant and procedures can contribute to higher levels of productivity

6. Farrell, M.J. (1957), *"The Measurement of Productive Efficiency"*, Journal of the Royal Statistical Society, Vol. 120, No.3, pp. 253-90.

Chapter - V

Conclusion and Recommendations

In the late 1980s, the emergence of the "new growth" theories yielded a rigorous analytical framework, where the liberalisation could be linked with economic growth. In particular, the impact of *Economic Openness* of any country brings technological changes in domestic technology, leading to the improvement in productivity, where the production process becomes more efficient. The liberalisation-productivity nexus for industrial sectors in developing countries was mixed. The empirical evidence on the impact of *Economic Openness* measures on the productivity performance for Indian industries was limited.

TFP growth increase is an important source of industrial growth. The empirical findings yield different results. Studies have projected lower TFP growth in domestic manufacturing sector. No rigorous empirical analysis has been undertaken to explain the poor productivity performance of Indian [domestic] manufacturing sector (Goldar, 1986). Little attention was being paid for the evaluation of the causes of change. The present study focuses on the industrial growth and the measurement of TFP growth. Hence, there is need to employ an appropriate methodology for analysing the performance of industry, particularly with respect to TFP and Growth Efficiency.

The study attempts to examine:

1. To analyse the growth performance of Gross Value Added [GVA], Capital and Labour in the selected industries.

2. To examine the TFP growth Pre and Post-Transition
3. To identify the sources of pre and post-transition TFP growth

Data Envelopment Analysis (DEA) approach-the Malmquist productivity Index (MPI) wase used to analyze TFP growth. It is a special mathematical linear programming model test to ascertain the efficiency and productivity, through panel data to estimate changes - breaking into technological change and technical efficiency change components. The present study endeavours to analyze the TFP growth trend in the domestic manufacturing sector based on technology classification as HT, MHT, LT, and MLTM sectors at both aggregated and disaggregated inter-industry levels. Using the Malmquist Productivity Index [MPI] for panel data set of 22 major industries was evaluated for about 31 years [1981-82 to 2011-12]. The TFP Change Index results were calculated by using Data Envelopment Analysis Programme 2.1 (DEAP) linear programme developed by Coelli *et.al* (1998).

Findings of the Study

Sector wise Growth Performance Analysis HTM Sector

- A comparative analysis of *pre and post-transition* period results indicated the growth rate trend of *GVA* [post-transition] as positive in the transition period and was positive for growth rate of *capital*, whereas that of *labour* as negative when compared to the pre-transition period.
- The disaggregate analysis results indicated all industries as positive [post- transition]. The highest growth rate of GVA was recorded by Radio, TV and Communication Industry and the lowest growth rate of GVA was posted by Drug and Medicines Industry [post-transition].
- Almost all industries recorded a positive growth rate of *Capital* [post-transition]. The maxima for the Office and Computing equipment Industry while the minima for Drugs and Medicines [post- transition in contrast with pre-transition].
- At the aggregate and disaggregate level, the growth of *labour* was lower than the Gross Value Added [GVA] and the Capital

in all the industries and the growth rate was found to be less than two per cent during the study period.

- The highest growth of *labour* was found in the Office and Computing equipment industry [post-transition]. Drugs and Medicines industry has scored the lowest growth of labour during transition period.
- The pre and post-transition growth at disaggregated industrial level depicted drastic decrease in growth of labour for all industries.

  However, the growth of GVA and Capital were positive [post-transition]. The reason may be the economic openness, with FDI inflow and the technology import, whereas, it was negative labour growth. HT sector were capital intensive for the lower utilization of labour, yielding to negative growth.

MHTM Sector

- GVA growth was positive in the tradition, whereas that of capital and labour stood negative [pre-transition compared with post-transition]. Five industries out of six industrial groups [pre-transition] accelerated with maxima for the other Transport Industry and minima for Non-electrical Industry [post-transition]..
- Post-transition growth of capital was maxima for professional goods and minima for the non-electrical goods [post-transition]. Almost all industries witnessed turn down in growth of capital [post-transition].
- Labour growth was lowest than GVA capital in industries during aggregated and disaggregated period. It was less than two per cent for almost all the industries.
- Labour growth was negative [pre-transition] for three industries out of six industrial groups, other than chemicals excluding drugs and other transport industries whereas the electrical machines excluding communication equipments, non-electrical and motor vehicles had negative labour growth [post-transition] in the accelerated growth drive.

The sector records positive GVA while that of capital and labour growth were negative [post-transition]. The scale of operation, as believed, was not optimal in resource utilization. The Economic Openness had adverse effect on the sector.

LTM Sector

- GVA decreased [post-transition w.r.t pre-transition] for food, beverages, tobacco industry posted maxima of 9.8 per cent growth [pre-transition], whereas wood products, furniture had minima of 1.8 per cent. But, post-1991, it has been reduced. The sector is labour intensive, but the result was negative despite positive belief.
- The capital growth slipped from17.5 per cent to10.3 per cent [post-transition].
- Almost all the industries reflected decrease in capital growth [post-transition]. Food, beverages and tobacco industries posted 18.5 per cent, while paper, paper products, printing reflected 15.6 per cent. The exercise went through the transition between pre-transition and post-transition.
- Labour growth was lower than GVA and capital at aggregate level of the study. A pre- and post-transition contrast yielded the growth of labour [post-transition] growth as negative with food, beverages and tobacco industries in the highest, whereas wood products and furniture had lowest growth.

The Economic Openness adversely effected GVA, capital and labour of the LTM sector. Pre-1991 industries were protected with Tariffs and Quantities Restrictions, but later, the EO get them reduced. So, labour-intensive industry expected positive but in vain.

MLTM Sector

A comparative analysis of pre and post-transition showed the GVA and capital growth to have decreased [post-transition] whereas that of labour growth was positive.

- GVA was maxima at 14.1 per cent [post-transition] for petroleum refineries and coal products whereas ship building and repairing of ships was minima at -12.1 per cent among eight shortlisted industries at the disaggregated level of study.

- Capital growth was maxima 25.1 per cent [pre-transition] for rubber, plastic products whereas ship building and repairing posted minima 1.1 per cent among inter-industry level study for the sector.
- Growth of labour [post-transition] was positive, from -0.9 per cent to 0.9 per cent for the sector at the aggregated study level.
- Labour growth posted maxima 8.4 per cent [post-transition] for other manufacturing industries and minima -7.5 per cent for non-ferrous industries among eight shortlisted industrial group for the sector.

MTML growth of GVA and capital was positive [pre-transition] and labour was negative in contrast with positive labour growth [post-transition] from the promotion of labour-intensive industries.

Sector wise findings - TFPG and Sources

HTM Sector

- TFPG was positive with the HTM sector at 1.004 during the study period.
- Economic Openness of TPG for the HTM showed -4.2 per cent [pre-transition] up to 3.0 per cent [post-transition]. Economic Openness affected as desired at the aggregated levels. It owed to technological changes.
- Office and computing equipments, radio and t.v. and communication equipments were efficient with TFPG at par or beyond with shifts in their frontiner on innovation [post-transition] whereas the drugs, medicines had declension. TFPG for office, computing industry posted 8.1 per cent and -4.6 per cent for drugs and medicines.

TFPG of HTMS owes to technological change and its import technology yielding desired results for Economic Openness [post-transition].

MHTM Sector

- TFP growth stood at 1.004 for the study period. Technological Change and Technological Efficiency change were equally contributing in the study period.
- It was -1.9 per cent [pre-transition] and 2.7 per cent [post-transition] due to Technological Change.
- At disaggregated level, all industries operated positively [post-transition] due to Technological Efficiency. The highest TFP growth was observed among the professional goods and other transport industry. The main source of TFP growth was technical efficiency change. Least efficient industry came to be non-electrical and the inefficient ones the electrical machines excluding communication equipment and motor vehicles.

The performance of MHTM sector owes to innovation or technological adoption yielding to shift ascendant of production frontier. TFP growth was positive [post-transition] due to improvement in techniques and production either by innovation or through technological adoptions among industries resulting in positive shift ascendant of production.

LTM Sector

- TFP stood negative under study period with index of 0.984 due to negative contribution from the change in technology, turned positive with an index value of 1.007. It reflects LTM sector operates at maximum potential output. Some industries still operate below maxima potential.
- The impact of Economic Openness here reveals that TFP growth fell from 1.2 per cent to -3.1 per cent [post-transition] on technological change but improved efficiency.
- Paper, and paper products, print industry reported highest productivity [contrast of post-transition with pre-transition] on technological change. The least efficient industries were wood products and furniture. Source of TFP growth was technological change. Least efficient industries were wood products and furniture.

The result reveals the growth in the industries was boosted by the productivity enhancement -based catching-up capability, specifically the effective use of human capital in the labour market. Though, the industries are capital-intensive (high expenses on physical asset) but, not optimally benefic from technological change.

MLTM Sector

- MLTM sector posted positive growth with an index of 1.007 during the study period upon technological change and technical efficiency change. Sources of TFP growth revealed that on average, both the technological change and technical efficiency change drove TFP growth.
- The impact of economic openness puts TFP growth positive, ranging from -0.8 per cent [pre-transition] to 2.4 per cent [post-transition]. At the aggregated level, economic openness impact was positive owing to the change in technology.
- The Inter-industry analysis reveals rubber and plastic products, other manufacturing industry, non-ferrous metals, non-metallic mineral products and petroleum refineries and coal products among eight shortlisted industries showed positive TFP growth [pre-transition]
- This indicates that the economic openness have adverse impact on particular industries productivity growth resulting declining in TFP growth [post-transition] The remaining industries post positive growth [post-transition] and owes to technical efficiency change.

At all aggregate levels, the technological change is greater than technical efficiency change, which implies that the growth in TFP was due to shift in the frontier rather than improvement in efficiency. Hence, the result projects a positive impact of economic openness on technological advancement in the sector

Recommendations and Policy implications

- HT, MHT, LT and MLT manufacturing sector are being classified on the basis of technology, whereas the labour growth finds neglected. Except, LT, all manufacturing sectors,

TFG growth attributes to the technological change. A strategic plan must be made to improve the labour efficiency through systematic advanced training programmes on imported technologies and continuous monitoring. India ought to utilize optimum human resources. India need to utilize human resources to the optimum level in all the four manufacturing process.

- LTM sector capital growth was low [post-transition]. Sufficient investment need to be made to improve the productivity.
- The research and development of four sectors are essential to improve the quality and quantity of products. Its impact not only increases productivity but optimum manpower utilization yields to TFP growth in industries.
- Each industry issue may be dealt separately with individual case to improve productivity. The weak industries need to be strengthened in the area. The government should frame special policies giving priority to those sectors.
- In low performing industries calling for the FDI inflow, the government need to promote them with suitable policies.
- The government should support the employment-intensive industries along with infrastructural facilities.
- For sustained environment, domestic industries and its besides their competitiveness in the international markets, there is an urgent need to adopt available new technologies across the world.

The above research highlights and projects about the existing reality of domestic manufacturing sectors classified on technology. It helps in understanding various industries upon growth, trends, structure, and industrial productivity performance. This research establishes a stronger foundation for advanced study at micro-economic level, leading to accelerate productivity, efficiency and boost the overall manufacturing sector.

Bibilography

Abhay Gupta (2009), "Looking Beyond the Methods: Productivity Estimates and Growth Trends in Indian Manufacturing University of British Columbia", *Munich Personal RePEc Archive* Paper No. 14482.

Agarwal, R.N. (2001b), *Technical efficiency and productivity growth in the central public sector enterprises in India during 1990s*, Discussion Paper 28/2001, Institute of Economic Growth, New Delhi.

Ahluwalia, I.J. (1985): "Industrial Growth in India - Stagnation since the Mid-Sixties", *OUP*, New Delhi.

Ahluwalia, I.J. (1991): *Productivity and Growth in Indian Manufacturing*, OUP, New Delhi.

Ahluwalia, Isher Judge and Little, I. M. D. (1998): " Introduction" in Ahluwalia, Isher Judge and Little, I. M. D. (eds.) (1998), *India's Economic Reforms and Development: Essays for Dr. Manmohan Singh,* OUP, Delhi.

Ahmed, S and Mathur, S.K. (2006): "Industrial sector Growth Accounting of Some Indian States and Union Territories: A Data Envelopment Analysis", *Foreign Trade Review*, Vol.40, No.40.

Ali Ugur (2004): "Technical Efficiency in Irish Manufacturing Industry, 1991-1999", Trinity College Dublin, Department of Economics series Paper with No. 20044.

Alternative Economics Survey, India 2012-13: Yuva Samvad Prakashan.

Anita Kumari (2005): "Liberalisation and Sources of Industrial Growth in India: An Analysis Based On Input-Output Approach" presentation at *15th International Input-Output Conference*, Beijing, China.

Annual Survey of Industries, [various issues up to 2012].

Arnab K. Deb (2011): "Economic Reforms and Total Factor Productivity Growth of Indian Manufacturing: An Inter-State Analysis", Brownbag Seminar Series, Department of Economics, University of Connecticut.

Arora, Vani and Singh, Parminder (2008): "Economic Reforms and Productivity Growth in Indian Manufacturing Sector: An Inter-state Analysis", *The ICFAI University Journal of Industrial Economics*, Vol. V, No. 3, pp. 35-47.

Asid, R (2010: "The Technical Efficiency Analyses of Manufacturing Sector in Malaysia: Evidence from the First Industrial Master Plan", *Asian Social Sciences,* Vol.6, No.2, pp.99 -107.

Atulan Guha (2008): "Evolution of Indian Organised Manufacturing Industrial Structure: A Comparison between Liberalised and Pre-liberalised Regimes", Conference paper, Institute for Studies in Industrial Development, New Delhi.

Balakrishnam, P. and K. Puspangadan (1996): "Total Factor Productivity Growth in Manufacturing Industry" *Economic and Political Weekly*, March 4.

Balakrishnan, P. and Pushpangadan, K. (1994:, "Total Factor Productivity Growth in Manufacturing Industry: A Fresh Look", *Economic and Political Weekly*, Vol. 29, No. 31, pp. 2028-35.

Beghels, L.M.S and Pendse (1997): "An Econometric Analysis of Productivity Growth and Technical Change in Total Manufacturing Sector of India," *The Indian Economic Journal,* Vol.44, No.2, pp.39-58.

Bjurek, Hans and Durevall, Dick (2000): "Does Market Liberalization Increase Total Factor Productivity? Evidence from the Manufacturing Sector in Zimbabwe", *Journal of Southern African Studies*, Vol.26, No.3 pp. 463-79.

Burange, L.G. (1999): "Industrial Growth and Structure: Manufacturing Sector in Maharashtra", *Economic and Political Weekly*, Vol.34, No.9, pp. M39-M48.

Chandrasekhar, C.P. (1988): "Aspects of Growth and Structural Change in Indian Industry", *Economic and Political Weekly*, Special Number, Vol.23, Nos.45-47, November, pp. 2359-70.

Charnes, A., Cooper, W. W., Lewin, A. Y., and Seiford, L. M. (1994): *Data Envelopment Analysis: Theory, methodology, and applications,* Boston: Kluwer.

Chattopadhyay, S.K. (2004): "Trends in Total Factor Productivity of Manufacturing Sector in West Bengal: A Sectoral and Temporal Analysis", *Reserve Bank of India Occasional Papers*, Vol.25. No.1.

Chaudhuri, Sudip (2002): "Economic Reforms and Industrial Structure in India", *Economic and Political Weekly*, Vol.37, No.2, January 12-18, pp. 155-62.

Coelli T.J, A Guide to DEAP Version 2.1: A Data Envelopment Analysis (computer program) CEAP working paper 96/08, Department of Econometrics, University of New England, Australia.

Corbo, Vittorio and Fischer, Stanley, (1995): "Structural adjustment, stabilization and policy reform: Domestic and international finance," Handbook of Development Economics, in: Hollis Chenery & T.N. Srinivasan (ed.), Handbook of Development Economics, edition 1, volume 3, chapter 44, pages 2845-24 Elsevier.

Dani Rodrik, (1993): "Trade and Industrial Policy reforms in Developing Countries: AReview of Recent theory and evidence"'National Bureau of Economoic research, Working Paper No 4417, Cambridge, New York.

Das, Santosh Kumar (2010): "Indian registered Manufacturing Sector: Changing Structure and Performance, 1980-04", *The IUP Journal of Managerial Economics,* Vol. VIII, No. 1&2.

Deb Kusum Das and Gunajit Kalita,(July 2009): "Aggregate Productivity Growth in Indian Manufacturing: An Application of Domar Aggregation", *Working Paper No. 239.* Indian Council For Research On International Economic Relations, New Delhi.

Dong-hyun, Oh (2011): "Productivity growth, efficiency change and technical progress of the Korean manufacturing industry", *Journal of the Asia Pacific Economy*, Vol.16, pp.1-5.

Ephraim W Chirwa (1998): "Technical Efficiency in Malawian Manufacturing Industries using the deterministic production frontier", University of Malawi, Department of Economics, *Working Paper WC/05/98.*

Ephraim W. Chirwa (2001): "Privatization and Technical Efficiency: Evidence from the Manufacturing Sector in Malawi", *African Development Review* Volume. 13 No. 2.

EPW Research Foundation (2002): Annual Survey of Industries, 1973-74 to 1997-98. A Data base on the Industrial sector in India, Mumbai.

Erumban A. A. (2005): "Economic Reforms and Industrial Performance: An analysis of Capacity Utilization in Indian Manufacturing", *Indian Journal of Economics and Business,* December, 4(2), pp. 305-223.

Fare, R., Grosskopf, S., Norris, M. and Zhang, Z. (1994): "Productivity Growth, Technical Progress and Efficiency Changes in Industrialized Countries", *American Economic Review*, Vol.84, pp. 66-83.

Farrell, M.J. (1957): "The Measurement of Productive Efficiency", *Journal of the Royal Statistical Society,* Vol. 120, No.3, pp. 253-90.

Fujita, N. (1994): "Liberalization Policies and Productivity in India" *The Developing Economies,* Vol. XXXII, No.4, December, pp.509-24

Fulwinder Pal Singh (2012): "Economic Reforms and Productivity Growth in Indian Manufacturing Sector – An Inter-State Analysis", *International Journal of Marketing, Financial Services & Management Research.* Vol.1, Issue 12.

Goldar, B. (1986), "*Productivity Growth in Indian Industry*", Allied Publishers, New Delhi.

Goldar, Bishwanath (2004): "Productivity Trends in Indian Manufacturing in the Pre- and Post-Reform Periods", *Working Paper no. 137*, Indian Council for Research on International Economic Relations, New Delhi.

Government of India (2011): The *National Strategy for Manufacturing*, National Manufacturing Competitiveness Council, New Delhi.

Grifell-Tatjé, E. and Lovell, C.A.K. (1995): "A Note on the Malmquist Productivity Index", *Economics Letters*, Vol. 47, No.2, pp. 169-75.

Gupta, Poonam and Kumar, Utsav (2010): "Performance of Indian Manufacturing in the Post-reform Period", *MPRA Paper No. 24898.*

Haishun Sun, Phillip Hone and Hristos Doucouliagos (1999): "Economic openness and technical efficiency: A case study of Chinese manufacturing industries", *Journal the Economics of Transition*, Volume 7(3):1999 pp: 615-36.

Hasan, R., D. Mitra, and K.V. Ramaswamy (2007): "Trade Reforms, Labour Regulations, and Labour-Demand Elasticities: Empirical Evidence from India," *Review of Economics and Statistics*, 89(3, August), pp. 466–81.

I.K.M. Mokhtarul Wadud (2007): "Productivity Growth and Efficiency Change in Malaysian Manufacturing: Recent Evidence from Disaggregated Data", School Of Accounting, Economics and Finance, Working *Paper* 2007 SWP 2007/12 Economic Series from Deakin University, Victoria.

India: Recent Economic Developments and Prospects, A World Bank Country Study, the *World Bank*, Washington DC 1995, p.43.

Industrial Policy Document 1991: Government of India.

J.C Sandesara, (1991): "New Industrial Policy: Questions of Efficient Growth and Social objectives," *Economic and Political Weekly*, August 3-10, 1991, page no.1870.

Jabir Ali, Surendra and E. Ekanem (2009): "Efficiency and Productivity Changes in the Indian Food Processing Industry: Determinants and Policy Implication" *International Food and Agribusiness Management Review* Volume 12, Issue 1.

Jad Chaaban, Vincent Réquillart and Audrey Trévisiol, (2005): "The role of technical efficiency in takeovers: Evidence from the French cheese industry, 1985–2000", *Journal of* Agribusiness, Volume 21, Issue 4, pp 545–64.

Jitender Singh, (2013): Analysis of Trends in the Manufacturing Growth in Last Five years, *Research Studies*, Office of the Economic Adviser, Department of Industrial Policy and Promotion, Ministry of Commerce and Industry, Government of India.

Joshi, V. and I.M.D. Little (1998): *India's Economic Reforms 1991-2001,* OUP, New Delhi.

Kalirajan, K. P. and Zhao, Shiji (1997): "Did the technical efficiency of state enterprises improve with the same speed in all provinces in China?" *Applied Economics*, 29, pp. 269-77.

Kankana, Mukherjee and Subhash, C. Ray (2005): "Technical Efficiency and its Dynamics in Indian Manufacturing: An Inter State Analysis", *Indian Economic Review*, Vol. 40, No.2, pp. 101-25, December.

Kiran, R. and Kaur, Manpreet (2007): "Is liberalization associated with Higher Productivity? A Case Study of Punjab Manufacturing Vision",*The Journal of Business Perspective*, Vol. 11, No. 4, Oct-Dec, pp. 53-64.

Kishor Sharma (2000): "Liberalization and Structural Change: Evidence from Nepalese Manufacturing", *Discussion Paper* NO. 812, Yale University and Charles Sturt University, Australia.

Kumar, M. and Basu, P. (2008): "Perspectives of Productivity Growth in Indian Food Industry: A Data Envelope Analysis", *International Journal of Productivity and Performance Management*, Vol.57, No.7, pp.503-522.

Kumar, S. (2001): "Explaining Inter-State Differentials in Total Factor productivity Growth in Indian Manufacturing Sector" *Indian Journal of Economics*, Vol. LXXXII, No.325.

Kumar,S.(2006):"Liberalization: Efficiency, Productivity and Production Function Behaviour in Indian Manufacturing Sector" *Indian Journal of Economics*, Vol. LXXXVI, No.344, pp.37-53.

Kumar, Sunil (2001): *Productivity and Factor Substitution- Theory and Analysis*, Deep and Deep Publishers Private Ltd, New Delhi.

Kumar, Surender (2004): "Decomposition of Total Factor Productivity growth: A regional analysis of Indian industrial manufacturing growth," *Working Papers 04/22*, National Institute of Public Finance and Policy.

Leachman, C., Pegels, C.C. and Shin, S.K. (2005): Manufacturing Performance: Evaluation and Determinants", *International Journal of Operations and Production Management*", Vol.25, No9, pp. 851- 74.

Mahadevan, R. (2001): "Assessing the Output and Productivity Growth of Malaysia's Manufacturing Sector", *Journal of Asian Economics*, Vol. 12, No. 4, pp. 587-597.

Mahadevan, R. (2002): "A DEA approach to understanding the Productivity Growth of Malaysia's Manufacturing Industries", *Asia Pacific Journal of Management*, Vol. 19, pp. 587–600.

Mandal,S.K.,Madheswaran,S.(2012):"Productivity growth in Indian cement industry: panel estimation of stochastic production frontier", Journal of Developing Areas, Vol. 46 No. 1, pp. 287-303.

Manjappa, D. H. and Mahesha, M. (2008): "Productivity Performance of Selected Capital Intensive and Labour Intensive Industries in India during Reform Period: An Empirical Analysis", *The ICFAI Journal of Industrial Economic,* Vol. V, No. 4, pp.57-65.

Manpreet and Ravi Kiran (2008): "Productivity Analysis of Indian manufacturing in pre- and post-liberalization era", *Journal of Contemporary Asia and Europe*, Volume I, No2, July-Dec, 2007 pp. 243-59.

Metin Karadag, A.Ozlem Onders and Ertugrul Deliktas (2005:, "Growth of Factor Productivity in the Turkish Manufacturing Industry at Provincial Level", *Regional Studies*, Taylor & Francis Journals, Vol. 39, No. 2, pp. 213-23.

Mookherjee, D. (1995): Indian Industry Policies and Performance, *OUP*, New Delhi.

Musleh–ud Din, Ejaz Ghani, and Tariq Mahmood (2007): "Technical Efficiency of Pakistan's Manufacturing Sector: A Stochastic Frontier and Data Envelopment Analysis", *The Pakistan Development Review* 46: 1, pp. 1–18.

Nagaraj, R. (2003): "Industrial Policy and Performance Since1980: Which way now?" *Economic and Political Weekly,* Vol.38, No.35, pp. 3707-15.

Nancy Kong and *Jose Tongzon* (2006): "Estimating Total Factor Productivity Growth in Singapore at sectoral level using data envelopment analysis" *Applied Economics*, 2006, vol. 38, issue 19, pages 2299-2314.

Nayyar, D. (1994): Industrial Growth and Stagnation: The Debate in India, OUP, New Delhi.

Neil Dias Karunaratne,(2007): "Microeconomic Reform and Technical Efficiency in Australian Manufacturing," *Discussion Paper*

No. 345, April 2007, School of Economics, The University of Queensland. Australia.

Nik Hashim Nik Mustapha and Basri Mohd Talib (2004): "Technical Efficiency and Total Factor Growth in Selected Malaysian Manufacturing Industries", proceeding Seminar Economic and Social Competitiveness Towards Strengthening Economic development, 11-13 June, 2004, Port Dickson Malaysia.

Nishimizu, M. and J.M. Page (1982: "Total Factor Productivity Growth, Technical Progress and Technical Efficiency Change: Dimensions of Productivity Change in Yugoslavia, 1965-78", *The Economic Journal*, 92 (368): 920-36.

Nizamettin B & Gokhan *D* (2008): "Performance Measurement of Turkish and Chinese Manufacturing Firms: A Comparative Analysis", *Eurasian Journal of Business and Economics*, Volume 1 (2), pp.71-83.

Parameswaran, M. (2002): "Economic Reforms and Technical Efficiency: Firm level Evidence from Selected Industries in India", *Working Paper 339*, Centre for Development Studies, Trivandrum, India.

Pradhan, G. and Barik, K. (1999): "Total Factor Productivity Growth in Developing Economies: A Study of Selected Industries in India", *Economic and Political Weekly*, July 31, M92-M97.

Raj, K.N. (1986): New Economic Policy, OUP, New Delhi.

Rajan, S.S, Reddy, K.L.N. and Pandit, V. (2008): "Total Factor productivity in selected Indian Manufacturing Industries" *The ICFAI Journal of Industrial Economics,* Volume No.1, pp. 51-78.

Rajesh Mehta (1997): "Trade Policy Reforms, 1991-92 to 1995-96- Their Impact on External Trade,"– ERP XXXII No. 15, April 12, 1997.

Randolph, B. and Campos, N. (2010): "The Growth Effect of Foreign Direct Investment in Low-Income Countries: A Meta-Regression Analysis of the Firm-Level Evidence," London, DFID Systematic Review Programme Report No. 1.

Ray, S.C. (2002): "Did India's Economic Reforms Improve Efficiency and Productivity? A Non-parametric Analysis of the Initial

Evidence from Manufacturing", *Indian Economic Review,* Volume. 37, No.1, pp. 23-57.

Ray, S.C. and Desli, E. (1997): "Productivity Growth, Technical Progress and Efficiency Change in Industrialized Countries: Comment", *American Economic Review*, Vol. 87, No. 5, pp. 1033-39.

Ray, Subash C. (1997),:"Regional Variation in Productivity Growth in Indian Manufacturing: A Nonparametric Analysis", *Journal of Quantitative Economics*, Volume.13, pp. 73-94.

Saba Vahid (2008): "Productivity Changes of the Wood Product Manufacturing Sector in the U.S.", *Applied Mathematical Sciences*, Volume. 2, 2008, no. 17, 799 - 816

Sahoo, Biresh K. (2008): "Decomposition of Total Factor Productivity Growth in Nonparametric Framework: A Reconsideration", *The Indian Journal of Economics*, Vol.XXXVIII, No.350, pp. 493-521.

Sanja S. Pattnayak, Thangavelu, S. M (2003): "Economic Reforms and Productivity growth in Indian Manufacturing Industries: An interaction of technical change and scale economies" *Working Paper* No. 0307, Department of Economics, National University of Singapore.

Sarbapriya Ray (2012): "Measuring and Decomposing Sources of Productivity Performance in India's Paper and Pulp Industry under Liberalized Regime: A Nonparametric Approach", *International Journal of Economic Sciences and Applied Research* 5 (1): 147-71.

Seekat, Khalid (2009): "Does Competition Improve Productivity in Developing Countries?" *Journal of Economic Policy Reforms*, Volume.12, No.2, pp.145-62.

Shalu Sehgal and Suparna Sharma (2011): "Total Factor Productivity of Manufacturing Sector in India: A Regional Analysis For The State Of Haryana", *Economic Journal of Development Issues* Vol. 13 & 14 No. 1-2.

Sidhu, Hena (2005b): "Inter- State Variations in factor productivity in the Indian Manufacturing sector during the post reform period", *Productivity*, Vol.46, No.1, pp. 54-62.

Srinivasan, T.N. and J. Bhagwati (1999): Outward-orientation and Development: Are Revisionists Right? Economic Growth Centre, Yale University, *Discussion Paper* No. 806.

Srivastava, V (1996): Liberalisation, Productivity and Competition: A Panel Study of Indian Manufacturing, *Oxford University Press*, and New Delhi.

Suwanee A. and Gavind C Reid (2009): "The Estimation of Technical Efficiency Effects Models with an Example Applied to the Thai Manufacturing Sector", *CRIEFF Discussion paper,* School of Economics & Finance, No. 0906.

Thomas, Jayan Jose. (2002): "A Review of Indian Manufacturing", in Parikh, Kirit and Radha Krishna, R (ed), India Development Report, 2002, New Delhi: Oxford University Press.

Trivedi Pushpa, Lakshmanan L., Jain Rajeev and Gupta Kumar Yogesh (2011): "Productivity, Efficiency and Competitiveness of the Indian Manufacturing Sector, *Development Research Group Study No.37*, Reserve Bank of India.

Uma Kapila (1992): "Recent Developments in India Economy", Part I edited by Uma Kapila, Academic, Foundation, 1992.

Unel, Bulent (2003): "Productivity trends in India's Manufacturing Sectors in the last two decades", Working Paper No.03/22, *IMF*, Washington University Press, New Delhi.

Unni Jeemol,, N. Lalitha and U. Rani (2001): "Economic Reforms and Productivity Trends in Indian Manufacturing", Economic and Political weekly Volume - XXXVI No. 41, October 13.

Virmani, Arvind and Hashim Danish A. (2009): "Factor Employment, Sources and Sustainability of Output Growth: Analysis of Indian Manufacturing", *Working paper No.3/2009*, Ministry of Finance, Government of India.

Appendices

ANNEXURE - I

Two- Digit Details of NATIONAL INDUSTRIAL CLASSFICATION (NIC) 1987

Sl. No.	***Major Industry Groups***
20-21	Food Products and other Food Products,
22	Beverages, Tobacco and Tobacco Products
23	Cotton Textiles
25	Jute, Hemp and Mesta Textiles
26	Other textiles (incl. Wearing apparel other than footwear
27	Wood and Wood Products, Furniture's and fixtures
28	Paper and paper products and printing industry
29	Leather, Leather and Fur Products (except repairs)
30	Chemicals & Chemical Products
31	Rubber, Plastic, Petroleum and Coal Products
32	Non-metallic Mineral Products
33	Basic Metal and Alloys Products
34	Metal Products and Parts (except Machinery & Transport)
35-36	Machinery and Equipments: Other than transport equipments
37	Transport Equipment and Parts
38	Other Manufacturing Industries

Source: MOSPI, New Delhi.

ANNEXURE - II

NATIONAL INDUSTRIAL CLASSFICATION (NIC 87)

Three Digit Codes and Description

Industry Code	*Group*	*Description of Industry*
Division		
20		**Manufacture of Food Products and 21 Manufactures of Other Food Products**
	200	Slaughtering, Preparation and Preservation of Meat
	201	Manufactures of Dairy Products
	202	Canning And Preservation of Fruits and Vegetables
	203	Canning, Preserving and Processing of Fish, Crustacea
	204	Grain Mill Products
	205	Manufactures of Bakery Products
	206	Manufactures And Refining of Sugar (Vacuum Pan Sugar Factories)
	207	Production of Indigenous, Sugar, From Sugar Cane, Palm Juice, Etc.
	208	Production of Common Salt
	209	Manufactures of Cocoa, Chocolate And Sugar Confactionary
	210	Manufacture of Hydrogenated Oils, Vanaspati Ghee, Etc.
	211	Manufacture of Edible Oils, Fats, Mustard Oil, Ground Nut Oil, Etc.
	212	Tea Processing
	213	Coffee Curing, Roasting And Grinding
	214	Cashewnut Processing Like Drying, Shelling, Roasting, Salting, Etc.
	215	Processing of Edible Nuts
	216	Manufacture of Ice
	217	Manufacture of Prepared Animal And Bird Feed
	218	Manufacture of Starch
	219	Manufacture of Food Products Not Elsewhere Classified
22		**Manufacture of Beverages,Tobacco and Tobacco Products**
	220	Distilling, Rectifying and Blending Of Spirits 3
	221	Wine Industries
	222	Malt Liquors and Malt
	223	Production of Country Liquor(Arrack And Toddy Etc)
	224	Manufacture of Soft Drinks And Syrups
	225	Tobacco Stemming, Redrying and All Other Operations Connected With Preparing Raw Leaf Tobacco

(Cont'd...)

	226	Manufacture of Bidi
	227	Manufacture of Cigars, Cigarettes, Cheroots And Cigarette Tobacco
	228	Manufacture of Chewing Tobacco,'Zarda'and'snuff' And Other Tobacco Products Nec(Except Pan-Masala Containing Tobacco
	229	Manufacture of Tobacco And Tobacco Products Not Elsewhere Classified
23		**Manufacture of Cotten Textiles**
	230	Cotton Ginning, Cleaning and Baling
	231	Cotton Spinning, Weawing, Shrinking, Sanforizing, Mercerising
	232	Printing, Dyeing And Bleaching of Cotton Textiles
	233	Cotton Spinning Other Than In Mills (Charkha)
	234	Production of Khadi
	235	Weaving and Finishing of Cotton Textiles In Handlooms, Other Than Khadi
	236	Weaving and Finishing of Cotton Textiles In Powerlooms
	239	Cotton Textiles Not Elsewhere Classified
24		**Manufacture of Wool, Silk and Synthetic Fibre Textiles**
	240	preparation of raw wool, silk and artificial/synthetic textile fibres for spinning
	241	wool spinning, weaving and finishing other than in mills.
	242	wool spinning, weaving and processing in mills
	243	dyeing and bleaching of woollen textiles
	244	spinning, weaving and finishing of silk textiles other than in mills
	245	spinning, weaving and processing of silk textiles in mills
	246	printing, dyeing and bleaching of silk textiles
	247	spinning, weaving and processing of man-made textiles fibres
	248	printing, dyeing and bleaching of artificial/synthetic textile fabrics
	249	silk and synthetic fibre textiles not elsewhere classified
25		**Manufacture of Jute and Vegetable Fibre Textiles(Except Cotton)**
	250	Jute and Mesta Pressing and Baling
	251	Jute and Mesta Spinning and Weaving
	252	Dyeing, Printing and Bleaching of Jute Textiles
	253	Preparing, Spinning, Weaving and Finishing Of Hemp And Other Coarse Fibre
	254	Spinning Weaving and Finishing of Jute And Mesta Textiles
	255	Spinning, Weaving and Finishing of Coir Textiles
	256	Spinning, Weaving and Finishing of Sann hemp And Other Vegetable Fibre Textiles Nec

(*Cont'd...*)

	257	Bleaching, Dyeing and Printing of Jute And Mesta Textiles
	258	Bleaching, Dyeing and Printing of Coir Textiles
	259	Bleaching, Dyeing and Printing of Other Vegetable Fibre Textiles Nec
26		**Manufacture of Textile Products (Including Wearing Apparel)**
	260	Manufacture of Knitted or Corcheted Textile Products
	261	Manufacture of All Types of Threads Cordage Ropes, Twine Nets Etc.
	262	Embroidery Work, Zari Work And Making Of Ornamental Trimmings
	263	263 Weaving Carpets, Rugs and Other Similar Textile Products
	264	264 Manufactures of Floor Coverings of Jute, Mesta Sann-Hemp And Other Kindred Fibres And of Coir
	265	Manufacture of Raincoats, Hats, Etc.
	266	266 Manufacture of Made Up Textile Goods such as Curtains, Mosquito Nets Etc.
	267	267 Manufacture of Water-Proof Textiles, such as Oil Cloth, Tarpaulin Etc.
	268	268 Manufactures of Waterproof Textile Fabrics
	269	Manufacture of Textiles Nec Like Linoleum, Padding, Wadding, Upholstering And Filling, Etc.
27		**Manufactures of Wood and Wood Products, Furniture and Fixtures**
	270	Sawing and Planning of Wood (Other Than Plywood)
	271	Manufacture of Veneer Sheets, Plywood and Their Products.
	273	Manufacture of Wooden and Cane Boxes Baskets and Similar Products Made From Bamboo And Reed, Etc.
	272	Manufactures of Structural Wooden Goods (Including Treated Timber)
	274	Manufacture of Wooden Industrial Goods Nec
	275	Manufacture of Cork And Cork Products
	276	Manufacture of Wooden Furniture And Fixtures
	277	Manufacture of Bamboo And Cane Furniture And Fixtures
	279	Manufacture of Products Of Wood, Bamboo, Reed, Grass And Cane
28		**Manufacture of Paper and Paper Products and Printing, Publishing and Allied Industries**
	280	Manufacture of Pulp, Paper And Paper Board, Including
	281	Manufacture of Containers And Boxes Of Paper Or Paper Board
	282	Manufacture of Paper And Paper Board Articles And Pulp Products Not Elsewhere Classified

(*Cont'd...*)

	283	Manufacture of Special Purpose Paper Whether Or Not Printed Nec.
	284	Printing And Publishing of Newspapers
	285	Printing And Publishing of Periodicals, Books, Journals, Directories Atlases, Maps, Sheet
		Music, Schedules And Pamphlets, Etc.
	286	Printing of Bank Notes, Currency Notes, Postage Stamps, Security Passes, Stamp Papers And Other Similar Products
	287	Engraving, Etching and Block-Making Etc.
	288	Books Binding On Account Of Others
	289	Printing And Allied Activities Nec
29		**Manufacture of Leather and Products of Leather, Fur Substitutes of Leather**
	290	Tanning, Curing, Finishing, Embossing and Japanning of Leather
	291	Manufacture of Footwear Except of Vulcanized Or Moulded Rubber Or Plastic
	292	Manufacture of Wearing Apparel of Leather And Substitutes of Leather
	293	Manufacture of Consumer Goods of Leather And Substitutes of Leather; Other Than Apparel And Footwear
	294	Scrapping, Currying, Tanning, Bleaching And Dyeing of Fur And Other Pelts For The Trade.
	295	Manufacture of Wearing Apparel of Fur And Pelts
	296	Manufacture of Fur And Skin Rugs And Other Similar Articles
	299	Manufacture of Leather And Fur Products Not Elsewhere Classified
30		**Manufacture of Basic Chemicals and Chemical Products (Except Products of Petroleum and Coal)**
	300	Manufacture of Indutrials Organic And Inorganic Chemicals (Manufacture Of Chemicals For Laboratory And Technical Uses Is Classified In 309.4
	301	Manufacture of Fertilizers And Pesticides
	302	Manufacture of Plastics In Primary Forms; Manufacture Of Synthetic Rubber
	303	Manufacture of Paints, Varnishes, And Related Products, Artists' Colours And Ink
	304	Manufacture of Drugs, Medicines And Allied Products
	305	Manufacture of Perfumes, Cosmetics, Lotions, Hailr Dressings, Toothplastes, Soap In Anyfor,
		Detetgents, Shampoos, Shaving Products, Washing And Cleanilng Preparations And Other Toilet Preparations
	306	Production of Man-Made Fibres

(Cont'd...)

	307	Manufacture of Matches
	308	Manufacture of Explosives; Ammunition And Fire-Works
	309	Manufacture of Chemical Products Nec
31		**Mfg of Ruubber,Plastic, Petroleum and Coal Products Processing of Nuclear Fuels**
	310	Tyres And Tubes Industries
	311	Manufacture of Footwear Made Primarily Of Vulcanized Ormoulded Rubber And Plastics
	312	Manufacture of Rubber Products
	313	Manufacture of Plastic Products Nec
	314	Manufacture of Refined Petroleum Products.
	315	Bottling of Natural Gas Or Liquified Petroleum Gas.
	316	Manufacture of Refined Petroleum Products N.E.C.
	317	Processing of Nuclear Fuels
	318	Manufacture of Coke Oven Products
	319	Manufacture of Other Coal And Coal Tar Products N.E.C.
32		**Manufacture of Non-Metallic Mineral Products**.
	320	Manufacture of Structural Clay Products
	321	Manufacture of Glass And Glass Products
	322	Manufacture of Earthenware And Plaster Products
	323	Manufacture of Non-Structural Ceramic Ware
	324	Manufacture of Cement, Lime And Plaster
	325	Manufacture of Mica Products
	326	Manufacture of Structural Stone Goods, Stoneware, Stone Dressing And Stone
	327	Manufacture of Asbestos Cement And Other Cement Products
	329	Manufacture of Miscellaneous Non-Metallic Mineral Products N.E.C.
33		**Basic Metal and Alloys Industries**
	330	Manufacture of Iron And Steel In Primary/Semi-Finished Forms
	331	Manufacture of Semi-Finished Iron And Steel Products In Rerolling, Cold Rolling,Wire- Drawing Mil
	332	Manufacture of Ferro-Alloys
	333	Copper Manufacturing
	334	Brass Manufacturing
	335	Aluminium Manufacturing Er Semi-Finished Products Of Aluminium N.E.C.
	336	Zinc Manufacturing
	337	Casting of Metals
	338	Processing/Re-Rolling Of Metal Scrap soother than Iron And Steel Scraps
	339	Other Non-Ferrous Metal Industries

(Cont'd...)

34		**Manufacture of Metal Products and Parts, Except Machinery & Equipment**
	340	Manufacture of Fabricated Structural Metal Products
	341	Manufacture of Fabricated Metal Products N.E.C.
	342	Manufacture of Furniture And Fixtures Primarily Of Metal
	343	Manufacture of Hand Tools And General Hardware
	344	Forging, Pressing, Stamping And Roll-Forming Of Metal, Powder Metallurgy.
	345	Treatment Or Coating Of Metals, General Mechanical Engineering On A Sub-Contract Basis.
	346	Manufacture of Metal Cutlery, Utensils And Kitchenware
	349	Manufacture of Metal Products Except Machinery And Transport
35&36		**Manufacture of Machinery and Equipment Other Than Transport Equipment**
	350	Manufacture of Agricultural Machinery And Equipment And Parts Thereof.
	351	Manufacture of Machinery And Equipment Used By Construction And Mining Industries.
	352	Manufacture of Prime Movers, Boilers And Steam Generating Plants And Nuclear Reactors
	354	Manufacture of Industrial Machinery For Other Than Food And Textile Industries
	355	Manufacture of Refrigerators, Air-Conditioners And Fire Fighting Equipment
	356	Manufacture of General Purpose Non-Electrical Machinery/ Equipment, Their Components
		and Accessories, Nec
	357	Manufacture of Machine Tools, Their Parts And Accessories
	358	Manufacture of Office Computing And Accounting Machinery And
	359	Manufacture of Special Plurpose Machinery/Equipment, Their Components And Accossories Nec
	360	Manufacture of Electrical Machinery,Apparatus, Appliance And Supplies.
	361	Manufacture of Insulated Wires And Cables
	362	Manufacture of Accumulators Primary Cells And Primary Batteries
	363	Manufacture of Electrical Lamps
	364	Manufacture of Electric Fans And Electric/Electro-Thermic Domestic Appliances And Parts Therof
	365	Manufacture of Apparatus For Radio Broadcasting Television Transmission
	367	Manufacture of Computers & Computer Basedsystems.

(*Cont'd...*)

	368	Manufacture of Electronic Valves & Tubes & Other Electronic Components Nec
	369	Manufacture of Radiographic X-Ray Apparatus,Tubes Parts & Manufacture Of Electrical Equipment Nec
37		**Manufacture of Transport Equipment and Parts.**
	370	Ship And Boat Building
	371	Manufacture of Locomotives And Parts
	372	Manufacture of Railway/Tramway Wagons And Coaches And Other Railroadequipment Nec.
	373	Manufacture of Heavy Motor Vehicles;Coach Works.
	374	Manufacture of Motor Cars & Other Motor Vehicles Principally Designed For The Transport Of Less Than 10 Persons
	375	Manufacture of Motor-Cycles & Scooters & Parts (Three-Wheelers)
	376	Manufacture of Bicycles,Cycle-Rickshaws & Parts
	377	Manufacture of Aircraft,Space Craft & Their Parts
	378	Manufacture of Bullock-Carts,Push-Carts & Hand-Carts Etc
	379	Manufacture of Transport Equipment & Parts Nec
38		**Other Manufacturing Industries**
	380	Manufacture of Medical, Surgical Scientific & Measuring Equipment Except Optical Equipment
	381	Manufacture of Photographic,Cinematographic & Optical Goods & Equipment
	382	Manufacture of Watches And Clocks
	383	383 Manufacture of Jewellery And Related Articles
	384	384 Minting of Currency Coins
	385	385 Manufacture of Sports And Athletic Goods
	386	386 Manufacture of Musical Instruments (Manufacture Of Toy Musical Instrument Is Classified In Group 389)
	387	Manufacture of Stationery Articles Nec
	388	Manufacture of Items Solars Cells,Cookers,Air And Water Heating Systems And Other Related Items
	389	Manufacture of Miscellaneous Products Nec
	390	Repair of Agricultural Machinery/Equipment
	391	Repair of Prime-Movers,Boilers,Steam-Generating Plants And Nuclear Reactors
	392	Repair of Machine Tools
	393	Repair of Industrial Machinery Other Than Machine Tools
	394	Repair of Office, Computing And Accounting Machinery
	395	Repair of Electrical Industrial Machinery And Apparatis
	396	Repair of Apparatus For Radio-Broadcasting Or Television Transmission: Radar, Radio Remote C Telephony
	397	Repair of Locomotives And Other Railroad Equipment
	398	Repair of Heavy Motor Vehicles
	399	Repair of Machinery And Equipment Nec

Source: MOSPI, New Delhi.

ANNEXURE- III

Two- Digit Details of National Industrial Classification (NIC) 1998

Sl. No.	***Major Industry Groups***
15	Manufacture of food products and beverages
16	Manufacture of tobacco products
17	Manufacture of textiles
18	Manufacture of wearing apparel; dressing and dyeing of fur
19	Tanning and dressing of leather; manufacture of luggage, handbags, saddlery,
20	Manufacture of wood and of products of wood and cork, except furniture;
21	Manufacture of paper and paper products
22	Publishing, printing and reproduction of recorded media
23	Manufacture of coke, refined petroleum products and nuclear fuel
24	Manufacture of chemicals and chemical products
25	Manufacture of rubber and plastics products
26	Manufacture of other non-metallic mineral products
27	Manufacture of basic metals
28	Manufacture of fabricated metal products, except machinery and equipment
29	Manufacture of machinery and equipment n.e.c.*
30	Manufacture of office, accounting and computing machinery
31	Manufacture of electrical machinery and apparatus n.e.c.
32	Manufacture of radio, television and communication equipment and apparatus
33	Manufacture of medical, precision and optical instruments, watches and clocks
34	Manufacture of motor vehicles, trailers and semi-trailers
35	Manufacture of other transport equipment
36	Manufacture of furniture; manufacturing n.e.c.
37	Recycling

Source: MOSPI, New Delhi.

ANNEXURE - IV

NATIONAL INDUSTRIAL CLASSFICATION (NIC) 1998

Divisions: Classification at two digit, three digit and four digit level

Industry Code	*Group*	*Class*	*Description*
15			**Manufacture of Food Products and Beverages**
	151		Production, processing and preservation of meat, fish, fruit vegetables, oils and fats.
		1511	Production, processing and preserving of meat and meat products.
		1512	Processing and preserving of fish and fish products
		1513	Processing and preserving of fruit and vegetables
		1514	Manufacture of vegetable and animal oils and fats
	152	1520	Manufacture of dairy product
	153		Manufacture of grain mill products, starches and starch products, and prepared animal feeds
		1531	Manufacture of grain mill products
		1532	Manufacture of starches and starch products
		1533	Manufacture of prepared animal feeds
	154		Manufacture of other food products
		1541	Manufacture of bakery products
		1542	Manufacture of sugar [manufacture of glucose and other sugars made fromstarches is classified in class 1532]
		1543	Manufacture of cocoa, chocolate and sugar confectionery
		1544	Manufacture of macaroni, noodles, conscious and similar farinaceous products
		1549	Manufacture of other food products n.e.c.
	155		Manufacture of beverages
		1551	Distilling, rectifying and blending of spirits; ethyl alcohol production fromfermented materials
		1552	Manufacture of wines
		1553	Manufacture of malt liquors and malt
		1554	Manufacture of soft drinks; production of mineral waters
16			**Manufacture of Tobacco Products**
	160	1600	Manufacture of tobacco products

(Cont'd...)

17			**Manufacture of Textiles**
	171		Spinning, weaving and finishing of textiles.
		1711	Preparation and spinning of textile fiber including weaving of textiles.
		1712	Finishing of textile.
	172		Manufacture of other textiles
		1721	Manufacture of made-up textile articles, except apparel
		1722	Manufacture of carpet and rugs
		1723	Manufacture of cordage, rope, twine and netting
		1729	Manufacture of other textiles n.e.c.
	173	1730	Manufacture of knitted and crocheted fabrics and articles
18			**Manufacture of Wearing Apparel; Dressing And Dyeing Of Fur**
	181	1810	Manufacture of wearing apparel, except fur apparel
	182	1820	Dressing and dyeing of fur; manufacture of articles of fur
19			**Tanning and Dressing of Leather; Manufacture of Luggage,Handbags Saddlery,Harness and Footwearc**
	191		Tanning and dressing of leather, manufacture of luggage handbags, saddlery & harness.
		1911	Tanning and dressing of leather
		1912	Manufacture of luggage, handbags, and the like, saddlery and harness
	192	1920	Manufacture of footwear.
20			**Manufacture Of Wood And Of Products Of Wood And Cork,Except Urniture;Manufacture Of Articles Of Straw And Plating Materials**
	201	2010	Saw milling and planing of wood
	202		Manufacture of products of wood, cork, straw and plaiting materials Manufacture of veneer sheets; manufacture of plywood, laminboard, particleboard and other panels and boards
		2021	Manufacture of veneer sheets; manufacture of plywood, laminboard, particleboard and other panels and boards
		2022	Manufacture of builders' carpentry and joinery

(Cont'd...)

		2023	Manufacturing of wooden containers
		2029	Manufacture of other products of wood, manufacture of articles of cork, straw andplaiting materials
21			**Manufacture of Paper And Paper Products**
	210		Manufacture of paper and paper product
		2101	Manufacture of pulp, paper and paper board
		2102	Manufacture of corrugated paper and paperboard and of containers of paper andpaperboard
		2109	Manufacture of other articles of paper and paperboard
22			**Publishing, Printing And Reproduction of Recorded Media**
	221		Publishing
		2211	Publishing of books, brochures, musical books and other publications
		2212	Publishing of newspapers, journals and periodicals
		2213	Publishing of recorded media
		2219	Other publishing [includes publishing of photos and postcards, time-tables, forms,posters or other printed matters.]
	222		Printing and service activities related to printing
		2221	Printing [Includes printing of newspapers, magazines, periodicals, journals andother material for others on a fee or contract basis]
		2222	Service activities related to printing
	223	2230	Reproduction of recorded media
23			**Manufacture of Coke, Refined Petroleum Products and Nuclear Fuel**
	231	2310	Manufacture of coke oven products
	232	2320	Manufacture of refined petroleum products
	233	2330	Processing of nuclear fuel
24			**Manufacture of Chemicals and Chemical Products**
	241		Manufacture of basic chemicals
		2411	Manufacture of basic chemicals except fertilizers and nitrogen compounds
		2412	Manufacture of fertilizers and nitrogen compounds
		2413	Manufacture of plastics in primary forms and of synthetic rubber.

(Cont'd...)

	242		Manufacture of other chemical products
		2421	Manufacture of pesticides and other agro chemical products
		2422	Manufacture of paints, varnishes and similar coatings,printing ink and mastics
		2423	Manufacture of pharmaceuticals, medicinal chemicals and botanical products
		2424	Manufacture of soap and detergents, cleaning and polishing preparations,perfumes and toilet preparations
		2429	Manufacture of other chemical product n.e.c.
	243	2430	Manufacture of man-made fibers
25			**Manufacture of Rubber And Plastic Products**
	251		Manufacture of rubber products
		2511	Manufacture of rubber tyres and tubes; retreading and rebuilding of rubber tyres
		2519	Manufacture of other rubber products
	252	2520	Manufacture of plastic products
26			**Manufacture of Other Non-Metallic Mineral Products**
	261	2610	Manufacture of glass and glass products
	269		Manufacture of non-metallic mineral products n.e.c.
		2691	Manufacture of non-structural non-refractory ceramic ware
		2692	Manufacture of refractory ceramic products
		2693	Manufacture of structural non-refractory clay and ceramic products
		2694	Manufacture of cement, lime and plaster
		2695	Manufacture of articles of concrete, cement and plaster
		2696	Cutting, shaping and finishing of stone
		2699	Manufacture of other non-metallic mineral products n.e.c.
27			**Manufacture of Basic Metals**
	271	2710	Manufacture of Basic Iron & Steel
	272	2720	Manufacture of basic precious and non-ferrous metals
	273		Casting of metals
		2731	Casting of iron and steel
		2732	Casting of non-ferrous metals

(Cont'd...)

28			**Manufacture of Fabricated Metal Products, Except Machinery and Equipments**
	281		Manufacture of structural metal products, tanks, reservoirs and steam generators
		2811	Manufacture of structural metal products
		2812	Manufacture of tanks, reservoirs and containers of metal
		2813	Manufacture of steam generators, except central heating hot water boilers
	289		Manufacture of other fabricated metal products; metal working service activities
		2891	Forging, pressing , stamping and roll-forming of metal; powder metallurgy
		2892	Treatment and coating of metals; general mechanical engineering on a fee or contract basis
		2893	Manufacture of cutlery, hand tools and general hardware
		2899	Manufacture of other fabricated metal products n.e.c.
29			**Manufacture of Machinery and Equipment N.E.C.**
	291		Manufacture of general purpose machinery
		2911	Manufacture of engines and turbines, except aircraft, vehicle and cycle engines
		2912	Manufacture of pumps, compressors, taps and valves
		2913	Manufacture of bearings, gears, gearing and driving elements
		2914	Manufacture of ovens, furnaces and furnace burners
		2915	Manufacture of lifting and handling equipment
		2919	Manufacture of other general purpose machinery
	292		Manufacture of special purpose machinery
		2921	Manufacture of agricultural and forestry machinery
		2922	Manufacture of machine-tools
		2923	Manufacture of machinery for metallurgy: converters, ingot moulds, ladles andcasting machines; metal rolling mills and rolls for such mills
		2924	Manufacture of machinery for mining, quarrying and construction

(Cont'd...)

		2925	Manufacture of machinery for food, beverage and tobacco processing
		2926	Manufacture of machinery for textile, apparel and leather production
		2927	Manufacture of weapons and ammunition
		2929	Manufacture of other special purpose machinery
	293	2930	Manufacture of domestic appliances, n.e.c.
30			**Manufacture of Office, Accounting and Computing Machinery**
	300	3000	Manufacture of office, accounting and computing machinery
31			**Manufacture of Electrical Machinery and Apparatus N.E.C.**
	311	3110	Manufacture of electric motors, generators and transformers
	312	3122	Manufacture of electricity distribution and control apparatus
	313	3130	Manufacture of insulated wire and cable
	314	3140	Manufacture of accumulators, primary cells and primary batteries
	315	3150	Manufacture of electric lamps and lighting equipment
	319	3190	Manufacture of other electrical equipment n.e.c.
32			**Manufacture of Radio, Television and Communication Equipment and Apparatus**
	321	3210	Manufacture of electronic valves and tubes and other electronic components
	322	3220	Manufacture of television and radio transmitters and apparatus for line telephony and line telegraphy
	323	3230	Manufacture of television and radio receivers, sound or video recording or reproducing apparatus, and associated goods
33			**Manufacture of Medical, Precision and Optical Instruments, Watches and Clocks**
	331		Manufacture of medical appliances and instruments and appliances formeasuring, checking, testing, navigating and other purposes except opticalinstruments
		3311	Manufacture of medical and surgical equipment and orthopedic appliances

(Cont'd...)

		3312	Manufacture of instruments and appliances for measuring, checking, testing,navigating and other purposes except industrial process control equipment
		3313	Manufacture of industrial process control equipment
	332	3320	Manufacture of optical instruments and photographic equipment
	333	330	Manufacture of watches and clocks
34			Manufacture of Motor Vehicles, Trailers and Semi-Trailers
	341	3410	Manufacture of motor vehicles
	342	3420	Manufacture of bodies (coach work) for motor vehicles; manufacture of trailers and semi-trailers
	343	3430	Manufacture of parts and accessories for motor vehicles and their engines
35			Manufacture of Other Transport Equipment
	351		Building and repair of ships & boats
		3511	Building and repairing of ships
		3512	Building and repairing of pleasure and sporting boats
	352	3520	Manufacture of railway and tramway locomotives and rolling stock
	353	3530	Manufacture of aircraft and spacecraft
	359		Manufacture of transport equipment n.e.c.
		3591	Manufacture of motorcycles
		3592	Manufacture of bicycles and invalid carriages
		3599	Manufacture of other transport equipment n.e.c.
36			Manufacture of Furniture; Manufacturing N.E.C.
	361	3610	Manufacture of furniture
	369		Manufacturing n.e.c.
		3691	Manufacture of jewellery and related articles
		3692	Manufacture of musical instruments
		3693	Manufacture of sports goods
		3694	Manufacture of games and toys
		3699	Other manufacturing n.e.c.
37			Recycling
	371	3710	Recycling of metal waste and scrap
	372	3720	Recycling of non-metal waste and scrap

Source: MOSPI, New Delhi.

ANNEXURE - V

Concordance between 4-Digit NIC-98 & 3-Digit NIC-87 (For Converting NIC-87 Based Data In Terms Of NIC98)

TABULATION CATEGORY D: MANUFACTURING

NIC98	*NIC-87*
1511	200
1512	203
1513	202
1514	210+211+212
1520	201
1531	204
1532	218
1533	217
1541	205
1542	206+207
1543	209
1544+1549	213+214+215+219
1551	220+223
1552	221
1553	222
1554	216+224
1600	225+226+227+228+229
1711	231+232+233+234+235+240+241+242+244+245+247+250 +251+252+253+254+255+256
1712	236+243+246+248+257+258+259
1721	267+268
1722	263+264
1723	261
1729	262+269
1730	260
1810	265+266+292+964
1820	294+295+296
1911	290
1912	293+299
1920	291+311
2010	270
2021	271
2022	272

(Cont'd...)

2023	273
2029	274+275+279
2101	280
2102	281
2109	282+283
2211+2219	285
2212	284
2213	Not defined separately in NIC-87
2221	286+289
2222	287+288
2230	Not defined separately in NIC-87
2310	318+319
2320	314+315+316
2330	317
2411	300
2412+2421	301
2413	302
2422	303
2423	304
2424	305
2429	208+307+308+309
2430	306
2511	310
2519	312
2520	313
2610	321
2691	322+323
2692+2693	320
2694	324
2695	327
2696	326
2699	325+329
2710	330+331+332
2720	333+334+335+336+338+339
2731+2732	337
2811	340

(Cont'd...)

2812	341
2813+2911	352
2891	344
2892	345
2893	343+346
2899	349
2912+2913+2914+2915	356+391
2919+2923+2927+2929	354+359+393+397+399
2921	350+390
2922	357+392
2924	351
2925+2926	353
2930	355+364+388
3000	358+367
3110+3120	360+395
3130	361
3140	362
3150	363
3190	369
3210	368
3220	365+396
3230	366
3311+3312+3313	380
3320	381
3330	382
3410+3420+3430	373+374
3511+3512	370
3520	371+372
3530	377
3591	375
3592	376
3599	378+379

(Cont'd...)

3610	276+277+342
3691	383+384
3692	386
3693	385
3694+3699	387+389
3710	Not defined separately in NIC-87
3720	Not defined separately in NIC-87

ANNEXURE - VI

Two- Digit Details of NATIONAL INDUSTRIAL CLASSFICATION (NIC) 2004

Industry Code No	*Major Industry Groups*
15	Food Products and Beverages
16	Tobacco Products
17	Textiles
18	Wearing Apparel; Dressing and Dyeing of Fur
19	Tanning and Dressing of Leather; Manufacture of Luggage, Handbags Saddlery, Harness and Footwear
20	Manufacture of Wood and of Products of Wood and Cork, Except Furniture
21	Paper and Paper Products
22	Publishing, Printing and Reproduction of Recorded Media
23	Coke, Refined Petroleum Products and Nuclear Fuel
24	Chemicals and Chemical, Products
25	Rubber and Plastic Products
26	Other Non-Metallic Mineral Products
27	Basic Metals
28	Fabricated Metal Products, Except Machinery and Equipments
29	Machinery and Equipment N.E.C.
30	Office, Accounting and Computing Machinery
31	Electrical Machinery and Apparatus N.E.C.
32	Radio, Television and Communication Equipment and Apparatus

(Cont'd...)

33	Medical, Precision and Optical Instruments, Watches and Clocks
34	Motor Vehicles Travellers' and Semi-Trailers
35	Other Transport Equipment
36	Furniture
37	Recycling

Source: MOSPI, New Delhi.

ANNEXURE-VII

Two- Digit Details of NATIONAL INDUSTRIAL CLASSFICATION (NIC) 2008

Industry	*Major Industry Groups*
Code No	
10	Manufacture of food products
11	Manufacture of beverages
12	Manufacture of tobacco products
13	Manufacture of textiles
14	Manufacture of wearing apparel
15	Manufacture of leather and related products
16	Manufacture of wood and products of wood
17	Manufacture of paper and paper products
18	Printing and reproduction of recorded media
19	Manufacture of coke and refined petroleum products
20	Manufacture of chemicals and chemical products
21	Manufacture of pharmaceuticals, medicinal chemical and botanical products
22	Manufacture of rubber and plastics products
23	Manufacture of other non-metallic mineral products
24	Manufacture of basic metals
25	Manufacture of fabricated metal products, except machinery and equipment
26	Manufacture of computer, electronic and optical products
27	Manufacture of electrical equipment
28	Manufacture of machinery and equipment n.e.c.
29	Manufacture of motor vehicles, trailers and semi-trailers

(Cont'd...)

30	Manufacture of other transport equipment
31	Manufacture of furniture
32	Other manufacturing
33	Repair and installation of machinery and equipment n.e.c.

Source: MOSPI, New Delhi.

ANNEXURE-VIII

Concordance between 4-Digit NIC-2008 & NIC 2004 (For Converting NIC-2004 based data in terms of NIC -2008)

NIC-2008	NIC-2004
1010	1511
1020	1512(p)
1030	1513(p)
1040	1514
1050	1520
1061	1531
1062	1532
1071	1541
1072	1542
1073	1543
1074	1544(p)
1075	1512(p)+1513(p)+1544(p)+1549(p)
1079	1549(p)+2429(p)
1080	1533
1101	1551
1102	0113(p)+1552
1103	1553
1104	1554
1200	1600
1311	1711(p)+1713(p)
1312	1711(p)+1713(p)
1313	1712+1714
1391	1730(p)

(Cont'd...)

1392	1721(p)+1722(p)+1725(p)
1393	1722(p)+1725(p)
1394	1723(p)
1399	1724+1729
1410	1810
1420	1820(p)
1430	1730(p)
1511	1820(p)+1911
1512	1912+3699(p)
1520	1920
1610	2010
1621	2021
1622	2022
1623	2023(p)
1629	2029(p)+3699(p)
1701	2101
1702	2102
1709	2109+3699(p)
1811	2221
1812	2222
1820	2230
1910	2310
1920	1010(p)+1020(p)+2320
2011	2330(p)+2411+2429(p)
2012	2412
2013	2413
2021	2421
2022	2422
2023	2424
2029	2429(p)
2030	2430
2100	2423
2211	2511
2219	2519(p)
2220	2520(p)
2310	2610(p)

(*Cont'd...*)

2391	2692
2392	2691(p)+2693
2393	2691(p)
2394	2694
2395	2695
2396	2696
2399	2699
2410	2711+2712+2713+2714+2715+2716+2717+2718+ 2719
2420	2720
2431	2731
2432	2732
2511	2811(p)
2512	2812(p)
2513	2813(p)
2520	2927(p)
2591	2891
2592	2892(p)
2593	2893(p)+2929(p)
2599	2899(p)
2610	3210(p)
2620	3000(p)
2630	3220(p)
2640	3230(p)
2651	3312(p)+3313(p)
2652	3330(p)
2660	3311(p)
2670	3312(p)+3320(p)
2680	2429(p)
2710	3110(p)+3120(p)
2720	3140(p)
2731	3130(p)
2732	3130(p)
2733	3120(p)
2740	3150(p)
2750	2930

(Cont'd...)

2790	3120(p)+3130(p)+3150(p)+3190(p)
2811	2911(p)
2812	2912(p)
2813	2912(p)
2814	2913(p)
2815	2914(p)
2816	2915(p)
2817	3000(p)
2818	2922(p)
2819	2919(p)
2821	2921(p)
2822	2922(p)
2823	2923(p)
2824	2924(p)
2825	2925(p)
2826	2926(p)
2829	2929(p)
2910	3410
2920	3420(p)
2930	3430
3011	3511(p)
3012	3512(p)
3020	3520(p)
3030	3530(p)
3040	2927(p)
3091	3591
3092	3592
3099	3599(p)
3100	3610
3211	3691
3212	3699(p)
3220	3692(p)
3230	3693
3240	3694(p)
3250	3311(p)+3320(p)
3290	3699(p)

(Cont'd...)

3311	2811(p)+2812(p)+2813(p)+2892(p)+2893(p)+ 2899(p)+
	2927(p)+2929(p)+3110(p)+3699(p)+7250(p)
3313	3220(p)+3311(p)+3312(p)+3313(p)+3320(p)
3314	2520(p)+3110(p)+3120(p)+3130(p)+3140(p)+ 3150(p)+ 3190(p)+3210(p)
3315	3511(p)+3512(p)+3520(p)+3530(p)+3599(p)+ 6303(p)
3319	1721(p)+1723(p)+2023(p)+2029(p)+2519(p)+ 2520(p)+
	2610(p)+2699(p)+3311(p)+3312(p)+3330(p)+ 3692(p)+3694(p)
3320	2813(p)+2911(p)+2912(P)+2914(p)+2915(p)+ 2919(p)+
	2921(p)+2922(p)+2923(p)+2924(p)+2925(p)+ 2926 (p)+
	2929(p)+3000(p)+3110(p)+3220(p)+3311(p)+ 3313 (p)

Index

A

A. Stephan, 39
Abhay Gupta, 31
African countries, 18
Ahluwalia, 22, 51
Ali Ugur, 38
Analysts Corbo, 19
Anita Kumari, 26, 28
Annual Survey of Industries (ASI), 45, 48
Arnab K. Deb, 33
Atulan Guha, 30
Audrey Trevisiol, 39

B

Balakrishnan, 51
Basri, 27
Battese, 38, 41
Board for Industrial and Financial Reconstruction (BIFR), 65
Brazilian, 27

C

Capacity Utilization (CU), 38
Center for Monitoring Indian Economy (CMIE), 50
Central Public Sector Enterprises (CPSE), 26
Central Statistical Organization (CSO), 48
China, 41, 60, 75
Coal products Industry, 88
Cobb-Douglas model, 34
Coelli, 38, 41

D

Data Envelopment Analysis (DEA), 28, 29, 30, 34, 93, 126
Data Envelopment Analysis, 39, 40
Deb Kusum Das, 32
Decision Making Units (DMUs), 93

E

E. Abdul Azeez, 38
E. Ekanem, 31
Ejaz Ghani, 40
Ephraim W. Chirwa, 36
Ephraim Wadonda Chirwa, 35
Ertugrul Deliktas, 28
Euler Pereira G., 27
Euro-Market, 62

F

Fischer, 19
Foreign Currency Convertible Bonds (FCCBs), 62
Foreign Direct Investment (FDI), 60, 61
Foreign Exchange Regulation Act (FERA), 57
Fulwinder Pal Singh, 33

G

G.V. Rama Krishna, 66

Gavind C Reid, 41

Global Depository Receipts (GDRs), 62

Gokhan D, 41

Gross Domestic Product (GDP), 17

Gross Value Added (GVA), 74

Gross Value Added, 29, 50, 82, 87, 88, 126

Gujarat, 33, 37

Gunajit Kalita, 32

H

Haishun Sun, 34

Haryana, 32

High Level Committee (HLC), 71

High Technology Manufacturing Sector, 81

Hristos Doucouliagos, 34

I

I.K.M. Mokhtarul Wadud, 29

Import liberalization, 24

Indian Industries Growth, 44

Indian Manufacturing Sector, 53

Indian Science and Technology Policy (ISTP), 45

Indonesia, 60

Industrial Entrepreneur Memorandum (IEM), 60

Industrial Licensing Policy, 59

Industrial Policy Resolution, 63

Integrated Industrial Townships, 70

Inter temporal Frontier, 36

International commercial banks, 18

International Monetary Fund (IMF), 18

J

J.C. Sandesara, 69

Jabir Ali, 31

Jad Chaaban, 39

Jose Tongzon, 29

K

Kalirajan, 34

Karnataka, 29

Kishor Sharma, 25

Kumar, 27

L

Latin American, 18

Least Developed Countries (LDCs), 44

M

M. Parameswaran, 37

Madhya Pradesh, 33

Mahadevan, 26

Majumdar, 92

Malawi, 36

Malawian, 35

Malaysian, 27

Malmquist Data Envelopment Analysis, 53

Malmquist Productivity Index (MPI), 30, 34, 52, 92, 126

Malmquist productivity Indices (MPIs), 29

Manufacturing Industry Promotion Board (MIPB), 70

Medium High Technology Manufacturing Sector, 85

Medium Low Technology Manufacturing Sector, 88, 90

Metin Karadag, 28

Michael. F, 39

Monopolies and Restrictive Trade Practices Act (MRTP), 22, 67, 70
Multi National Enterprises (MNE), 36
Musleh–ud Din, 40

N

N. Lalitha, 37
Nancy Y. C. Kong, 29
National Investment and Manufacturing Zones (NIMZ), 70
National Manufacturing Policy (NMP), 70
Neil Dias Karunaratne, 40
Nepal, 25
New Industrial Policy (NIP), 57
Nik Hashim, 27
Nizamettin B, 41
Non Resident Indian (NRI), 58

O

Oleg Badunenko, 39
Orissa, 33

P

Pakistan, 40, 75
Pattnayak, 26
Perpetual Inventory Accumulation Method (PIAM), 51
Phillip Hone, 34
Public Private Partnership (PPP), 70
Public Sector Enterprises (PSEs), 66
Pushpangadan, 51

R

R. Macedo, 27
R.N. Agarwal, 25
Rajasthan, 33
Rajesh Mehta, 24
Rakesh Mohan, 66
Ravi Kiran, 25
Rodrik, 43

S

S. Madheswaran, 32
Saba Vahid, 30
Sabuj Kumar Mandal, 32
Sanja S., 26
Secretariat for Industrial Approvals (SIA), 60
Securities and Exchange Board of India (SEBI), 62
Seemingly Unrelated Regression Estimation (SURE) technique, 38
Shallu Sehgal, 32
Sick Industrial Companies Act, 65
Singapore, 29
South Korean, 26
Stochastic Frontier Approach, 32
Structural Adjustment Program (SAP), 18
Suparn Sharma, 32
Surender, 27, 31
Suwanee A., 41

T

Taiwan, 60
Tariq Mahmood, 40
Technical Efficiency Change (TEC), 32
Technical Efficiency Change, 93, 105, 123
Technical Efficiency, 25
Technological Change, 93, 123
Thailand, 60
Thangavelu, 26
Tobacco Industry, 85, 87, 111, 128
Total Factor Productivity (TFP), 32, 33, 52, 92

Total Factor Productivity Change Index, 92
Total Factor Productivity, 94
Turkey, 28, 41

U

U. Rani, 37
Unni Jeemol, 37
Uttar Pradesh, 33

V

V. Krishnamurthy Committee, 66
Vincent Requillart, 39

W

World Bank (WB), 18

Z

Zhao, 34